How to Earn More Money as a Freelancer in a Gig Economy

V. V. CAM

ISBN-13: 978-0-9959387-3-1

CONTENTS

WHY THIS BOOK EXISTS

The gig economy is part of a shifting cultural and business environment. According to Investopedia.com (http://www.investopedia.com/terms/g/gig-economy.asp), "In a gig economy, temporary, flexible jobs are commonplace and companies tend toward hiring independent contractors and freelancers instead of full-time employees. A gig economy undermines the traditional economy of full-time workers who rarely change positions and instead focus on a lifetime career."

In my book, *Because Money Matters: The 8 Principles to Build Your Wealth* (http://www.because.zone/because-money-matters), I outlined eight principles for building wealth. The first principle is about earning as much as possible. Running a freelancing business is one of many ways to do so. This book fulfills my promise to share how I became a Top Rated Seller on Fiverr.com (https://www.fiverr.com) and added about $10,000 each year for the past five years to my full-time income by working less than five hours a week in my spare time in the evenings and weekends.

I chose to freelance because I wanted to earn as much as I could while I can. I also wanted to have an option to earn extra money doing something I enjoy after I retire in a few years. I researched freelancing opportunities and signed up on Fiverr.com in September 2012 to provide Adobe Portable Document Format (PDF) form design services. Since then, with many mistakes made and a few lessons learned, I've completed over 1,500 orders ranging from $5 to $1,800, received over 1,000 five-star reviews, gained many happy repeat clients, and made a few friends along the way. I've also contributed my thoughts on Fiverr's forum, created free tools for sellers and buyers, and offered free promotions on my website to fellow sellers.

Fiverr chose me as one of their Top Rated Sellers in February 2015. This status is given to sellers who maintain high standards and high ratings, deliver on time, and play fair. Top Rated Sellers enjoy a growing number of exclusive benefits, such as the ability to offer additional services for higher amounts, get faster support, and the chance to receive early access to beta features.

Being a seller on Fiverr.com has given me opportunities to help and interact with people all over the world. The extra money I've earned has also helped my husband and me in publishing and marketing our books (http://www.because.zone).

The potential to earn income as a freelancer is based on your ability, effort, and time. The Design Salary Guide (http://www.coroflot.com/designsalaryguide) provides real-time compensation information for design and creative professionals around the world. Many sellers on Fiverr.com earn six-figure income.

I've learned a lot about the freelance world. I want to share my knowledge, my experience and the lessons I've learned with you. I've also included tips, tools, and samples to help you along the way.

Running a single-person freelancing business requires a variety of skills and abilities. I've chosen to focus this book on earning money by attracting and retaining clients, because without clients, your business cannot make money. As a result, this book will not provide how-to information about registering your business, writing contracts, issuing invoices, keeping records, or filing taxes.

This book will show you what you need to get started as a freelancer, especially if you want to run your business on Fiverr.com. If you are a freelancer wishing for better success, this book will help you get to the next level where you get paid top dollar and have the freedom to choose clients and projects.

This book is about my experience on Fiverr.com. Because the platform changes frequently, it does not include step-by-step instructions, but it describes Fiverr's process and includes information that can be used on similar freelance websites.

I am confident this book gives you all the tools and inspiration you need to be successful in this gig economy, whether you are a part-timer new to freelancing or an experienced freelancer working full-time.

After reading this book, you will know:

- The advantages and disadvantages of being a freelancer and whether a freelancing business is right for you.
- How to find out what you want to do.

- What it takes to become a successful freelancer earning his/her worth.
- Where and how to set up your online shop for your freelancing business.
- How to price your service using the C.O.S.T. model to reflect the true value of your expertise and the work you do.
- How to get and retain clients and referrals through excellent client service.
- How to properly manage your business without stress while staying competitive, current, and relevant.
- How to use the BASIC test to ensure the effectiveness and professionalism of your written communication.
- How to handle different types of clients.
- How to use the 48 ready-to-use message templates to communicate and negotiate effectively with clients in various scenarios.

Ready? First, please let me explain what freelancing is about.

BECOMING A FREELANCER

A freelancer or freelance worker (also sometimes referred to as an independent contractor) is a person who is usually self-employed and is not necessarily committed to a particular employer. Some freelance workers are represented by a company or a temporary agency that resells freelance labour to clients. Some freelancers work independently and promote their business themselves while others use professional associations or websites to get work.

This book focuses on running a business as an independent freelancer who uses websites to offer his/her work. It is different from using websites where freelancers bid for work posted by buyers.

The regularity and type of freelance work can vary. A freelancer often offers various types of services to multiple businesses and individuals concurrently.

While the marketplace of freelancers is competitive, the need for quality and reliable freelancers is growing. Being a freelancer can be a great way to earn money while gaining experience, testimonials, and referrals.

Here are the main advantages and disadvantages of using other companies' websites to offer work:

1.1 Advantages

- You can get started quickly if you know what you want to do and have the necessary skills.
- Your business starts in an established marketplace.
- You don't have to build and maintain your own infrastructure, website traffic, and money management system.
- You can choose your place of work and you can set your own hours, working full or part-time on the projects of your choice.

- You can control how the work is done to fulfill your clients' specifications.
- You can set your own price.
- You don't have to chase clients for payments after an order is completed and closed.

1.2 Disadvantages

- It can be difficult to gain visibility in a competitive marketplace.
- It can take time to build a steady clientele.
- Work can be irregular. You will need to plan for slow times and be ready to work hard to deliver work on-time when work is plentiful.
- Managing multiple clients and projects can be a challenge.
- You don't receive benefits such as vacation or sick pay.
- You have to operate within the website's terms of service which can be restrictive, for example, you can communicate or accept payments only through the methods provided by the website.
- You are dependent on the website that keeps all the information about you and your clients.

Take the following self-assessment to see if you are ready to run your own freelancing business. Since it is a business, there will be more responsibilities than working as an employee. You will be responsible for other things that come with starting a business, such as keeping proper business records, complying with legal requirements, obtaining appropriate insurance, and reporting of business taxes.

1.3 Self-Assessment: Am I ready to be a freelancer?

Select all the statements that apply to you:

☐ I know what service I want to provide.

☐ I read, write, and understand English.

☐ I have the core skills required for the service that I plan to provide.

☐ I am self-motivated.

☐ I am organized.

☐ I can keep good records.

☐ I am able and willing to learn and improve.

☐ I can work alone without supervision or with others.

- ☐ I have a place to work.
- ☐ I have all the required tools and equipment, for example, computer, software and anything else I need to run my business.
- ☐ I have computer skills including uploading/downloading files and creating videos.
- ☐ I have access to the Internet.
- ☐ I know how to use Internet communication tools, for example, email and Skype.
- ☐ I have an account for receiving money, for example, PayPal or bank account.
- ☐ I have an email account.
- ☐ I am prepared to build a portfolio of my work to use as samples.
- ☐ I am able to recognize and correct my mistakes.
- ☐ I am able to consider consequences and make effective, clear decisions.

- ☐ I have checked into how freelancing would affect my income tax situation.
- ☐ I have checked into whether I need and can get appropriate licence or permit for my business.
- ☐ I have checked into whether I need and can get insurance or bond for my business.
- ☐ I know what is involved in running a small business.
- ☐ My family and friends are supportive of my work (if applicable).

Downloadable Item
1.3 Self-Assessment: Am I ready to be a freelancer? **Log in:** https://goo.gl/MXjBmM or **Sign up:** https://goo.gl/xpPbNM

Ideally, you would have checked off all the items above. If not, now is the time to get prepared.

Below are some freelance fields, services, and websites you may want to explore. You can also check out freelance websites for more ideas.

1.4 List of freelance fields

- Technical writing
- Copywriting and editing
- Project management
- Consulting (strategic, accounting, management, IT, tax, marketing, fashion/image)
- Business writing (business plans, grants, white papers, proposals)
- Sales
- Public relations
- Research
- Transcription services
- Career help (finding work, optimizing resumes, cover letters, interviews)
- Event planning/Event promotion
- Video production and editing
- Design (brochures, business cards, logos, newsletters, forms, presentations)
- Web design and development

- Audio production and mastering
- Photography
- E-commerce (Search engine optimization (SEO), Pay-per-click advertising (PPC), Google Analytics, lead generation)
- Blogging
- Test preparation help
- Productivity coaching
- Sports/Personal training
- Business training
- Martial arts instruction
- Dance/Choreography instructing
- Dating/Social skills coaching
- Music teaching
- Accounting/Bookkeeping
- Tax and financial planning
- Travel planning
- Personal/Virtual assistant
- General computer help and training.

1.5 Sample services

Graphics & Designs

- Design logos, posters, banners, book covers, business cards and stationery, postcards, pamphlets, invitations, T-Shirts, business forms…
- Design mobile apps
- Illustrate characters, create cartoons, caricatures…
- Create 3d rendering and animation of products
- Create presentations and infographics
- Graphic editing, manipulation, and vector tracing
- Create digital photo albums and scrapbooks

Marketing

- Create Facebook landing pages
- Drive targeted traffic to websites
- Submit press releases, articles, web links to agencies or directories
- Promote services and products through email, Short Message Service (SMS), social media, videos, human billboards, audio broadcast…

- List businesses on local directories
- Set up Facebook or Google AdWords campaigns
- Set up Google Analytics.

Writing & Translation

- Write, edit, or proofread articles, blog posts, letters, emails, product descriptions, resumes, cover letters, press releases, copywriting, research papers, summaries, contracts, terms and conditions…
- Review, edit, or critique resumes, cover letters, profiles, presentation…
- Translate or transcribe texts, audios, and videos from one language to another.

Audio, Video & Animation

- Edit video files
- Mix and master audio files
- Create animation for games and apps
- Create videos for sales, explainer, product demo, spokesperson, intros, animated logos…

- Compose and record music, songs, jingles, DJ drops, sound effects… for different purposes or occasions
- Record voiceovers for videos.

Programming & Tech

- Create or edit spreadsheets and databases
- Build, customize, secure, or fix websites
- Critique websites
- Provide remote technical support
- Install and configure web software
- Backup, clone, or migrate websites
- Generate Search Engine Optimization (SEO) reports for websites
- Conduct user tests for websites and apps
- Develop custom applications and bots
- Conduct data, statistical, or mathematical analysis
- Perform data entry, scraping/mining, mapping, visualization, modeling…
- Convert files to different formats
- Create custom database queries.

Business

- Perform virtual assistant tasks: data entry, administration and support, research…
- Research markets, products, keywords, names…
- Prepare business plans
- Consult on legal issues and applications
- Provide bookkeeping and accounting services.

Other

- Provide online lessons or advice on school subjects, music, relationships, health, nutrition, fitness…
- Provide psychic readings or spiritual teachings
- Perform genealogy researches and create family trees
- Help others get better at playing games.

1.6 How to find what you want to do

With so many fields and services to choose from, finding something to focus on can be overwhelming. Use these questions or the worksheet method below to help find what you want to do:

- What am I good at?
- What do I enjoy doing?

- What am I passionate about?
- What skills, talents, abilities make me stand out?
- What can I do with the skills and talents I have?
- What am I interested in?
- What do my friends call me for advice on?
- What motivates me?
- What opportunities do I see?
- What's trending?
- Where could I join for discussions and to get ideas?
- What am I known for, and fabulous at?
- What can I offer and do that is significantly different from what is currently available?
- What was I noticed for when I was younger?
- What life experiences have shaped me in special ways?
- What are my life purposes?

Worksheet: How to find what to do

Step 1

On a piece of paper, list three to ten skills, experiences, or interests you have that complete one of these two statements "I am great at…" or "I love to…"

Let's say your list looks like this:

1. I am great at typing.
2. I love to talk to people.
3. I love to solve problems.
4. I am great at finding information on the Internet.
5. I love to write.
6. I love to help people.
7. I am great at explaining things.
8. I love to keep things organized.
9. I love to teach.
10. I am great at speaking in front of people.

Step 2

Sort the above list based on how much you enjoy doing the tasks. For example, if you enjoy writing the most and typing the least, your sorted list would look something like the following:

1. I love to write.
2. I love to talk to people.
3. I love to help people.
4. I love to teach.
5. I am great at speaking in front of people.
6. I am great at explaining things.
7. I love to solve problems.
8. I am great at finding information on the Internet.
9. I love to keep things organized.
10. I am great at typing.

Step 3

Write below each of the top three items the three things you could and want to do with that skill or interest. Start each statement with "I can". For example:

1. I love to write:
    - I can write articles.
    - I can write web content.
    - I can ghostwrite novels.

Now you have nine things you can do. These are the things you'd enjoy doing because you have the passion and capacity to do them well. Pick the one that you are able to start right away. The field or service you choose for now may not be your top choice, but you can always come back and pick another one from this list when you are ready.

Downloadable Item
1.6 Worksheet: How to find what to do **Log in:** https://goo.gl/MXjBmM or **Sign up:** https://goo.gl/xpPbNM

1.7 List of freelance websites

These websites are similar to Fiverr.com. They allow freelancers to post their service for buyers to buy.

- Freelancer

  http://www.freelancer.com

- Guru

  http://www.guru.com

- iFreelance

  https://www.ifreelance.com

- People per Hour

  https://www.peopleperhour.com

- Shopify Experts

  https://experts.shopify.com

- Toptal

  https://www.toptal.com

- Upwork

  http://www.upwork.com

1.8 Other freelance websites/job boards

These websites allow buyers to post jobs for freelancers to apply. Check out http://nation1099.com/freelance-websites-need-know for more.

- 99designs

  https://99designs.ca

- Freelance Writing Jobs

  http://www.freelancewritinggigs.com

- Smashing Jobs

  https://jobs.smashingmagazine.com/freelance

- Working Nomads

  https://www.workingnomads.co/jobs

1.9 Checklist: Selecting a freelance website

Use this checklist to compare and find a suitable website where you want to set up your freelancing business:

	Website Name	Website Name	Website Name
Does it have good reviews and recommendations?			
Is it professional and easy to navigate?			
Does it look like an active website? For example, dates are current and a high number of postings.			
Is the level of support high so I can get started quickly?			
What methods of support (e.g. email, online chat, phone, forum, etc.) are available?			

	Website Name	**Website Name**	**Website Name**
Are there helpful tutorials available?			
Am I satisfied with the fees?			
Does it provide various functions and tools that I need?			
Is the dashboard user-friendly?			
What can I customize?			
Is it easy to set up shop?			
Can I use it on all my operating systems and devices?			
Does it have a good search engine?			
Does it have a payment method and currency that I want?			
Does it provide useful reports and statements?			

	Website Name	Website Name	Website Name
Will it allow videos, photos, documents, and links to external websites?			
What are the extra features? Will I be using them? Do they cost extra?			
Does the website make regular upgrades (check its announcements through newsfeed, blogs, or forum)?			

Downloadable Item
1.9 Checklist: How to select a freelance website **Log in:** https://goo.gl/MXjBmM or **Sign up:** https://goo.gl/xpPbNM

FREELANCING ON FIVERR.COM

Founded in 2010, Fiverr.com is a global online marketplace offering a few million services and products (such as handmade crafts and premade electronic document templates) for people to buy and sell.

Starting your business through a website like Fiverr.com is quicker than building and maintaining your own infrastructure, clientele, website traffic, and money management system. As soon as you sign up, you get access to everyone who uses the platform. Your service or product gets seen by many people, including users that are not directly looking for your service or product.

Since people are going to hire you as an expert or at least as someone experienced, you will need to work towards mastering the core skills behind the services you provide. For example, a web software developer will need to know technical terminology, programming languages, and how to build web applications. An editor will need to know the language's vocabulary, punctuation, and grammar rules besides knowing different types of writing.

In this chapter, let's go through how to get started working as a freelancer on Fiverr.com. The process includes these steps:

1. Setting up shop
2. Getting orders
3. Working on orders
4. Delivering work
5. Getting ratings, reviews, and tips (optional)
6. Getting paid.

STEP 1: SETTING UP SHOP

2.1 How Fiverr.com works

Fiverr.com does not require a subscription or fees to list your services or products. Each type of service or product is referred to as a Gig. The term "Gig" is also used to represent $5 USD (hence the name Fiverr).

There are over 100 categories (https://www.fiverr.com/categories) and you can offer any Gig you wish as long as it's legal and complies with Fiverr's terms. You can set your pricing anywhere from $5 to $995 and offer up to three versions (also referred to as Packages) of your Gig at three different prices. In addition, you can send Custom Offers up to $10,000 each.

Only registered users can buy and sell on Fiverr.com so to start selling, you will need to:

1. Create an account (https://sellers.Fiverr.com/en/article/creating-an-account)
2. Create a seller profile (https://sellers.Fiverr.com/en/article/creating-your-seller-profile)
3. Create your Gig(s) (https://sellers.Fiverr.com/en/article/creating-a-gig).

Buyers and sellers communicate through Fiverr's internal messaging system. As a seller, you can contact other sellers at any time for inquiries or to purchase their service, but you can only communicate with buyers after they contact you first.

Fiverr makes money by charging sellers 20% of their sales and buyers a small processing fee. Buyers who purchase your Gig pay Fiverr in advance. After you successfully deliver your order and the buyer rates it or the system automatically marks the order complete after three days, you will receive 80% of the total order value. Money you earned will be kept in your Fiverr account up to two weeks before you can withdraw it.

Sellers can obtain different levels based on their performance, level of service, and sales (https://www.fiverr.com/levels).

Level	**Requirements**
New	• You are automatically a New Seller once you join Fiverr.com.
Level 1	• Complete at least 60 days as an active Seller on Fiverr • Complete at least 10 individual orders • Earn at least $400 • Maintain a 4.8-star rating over the course of 60 days • 90% Response rate over the course of 60 days

Level	Requirements
	• 90% Order completion over the course of 60 days • 90% On-time Delivery over the course of 60 days • Not receiving warnings on violating Terms of Service over the course of 30 days • This is an automatic process based on the seller's past 60 days performance.
Level 2	• Complete at least 120 days as an active Seller on Fiverr • Complete at least 50 individual orders • Earn at least $2,000 • Maintain a 4.8-star rating over the course of 60 days • 90% Response rate over the course of 60 days • 90% Order completion over the course of 60 days • 90% On-time Delivery over the course of 60 days • Not receiving warnings on violating Terms of Service over the course of 30 days • This is an automatic process based on the seller's past 120 days performance.

Level	Requirements
Top Rated	• Complete at least 180 days as an active Seller on Fiverr • Complete at least 100 individual orders • Earn at least $20,000 • Maintain a 4.8-star rating over the course of 60 days • 90% Response rate over the course of 60 days • 90% Order completion over the course of 60 days • 90% On-time delivery over the course of 60 days • Not receiving warnings on violating Terms of Service over the course of 30 days • Once all requirements are met, Fiverr.com reviews your performance then manually selects and confirms status.

Depending on the level, sellers receive certain benefits and are allowed to post a select number of Active Gigs, Gig Extras (additional services within the same Gig) and Gig Multiples (multiple quantities of the same Gig).

For example, if a seller offers a black-and-white caricature (head and shoulders) drawing for $25, he/she could create two Gig Extras: One for a full body caricature for an additional $15 and the other for a coloured caricature for an additional $20.

If a seller offers a logo design for $10, a buyer who needs two different logos can order the Gig twice (for $20) through Gig Multiples.

Level	**Benefits**
New	• 7 Active Gigs • 2 Gig extras ($5, $10, $20) • 5 Gig Multiples • Send Custom Offers, up to $5,000 • Earning clearance: 14 days
Level 1	• 10 Active Gigs • 4 Gig Extras ($5, $10, $20, $40) • 10 Gig Multiples • Send Custom Offers, up to $5,000 • Earning clearance: 14 days

Level	Benefits
Level 2	• 20 Active Gigs • 5 Gig Extras ($5, $10, $20, $40, $50) • 15 Gig Multiples • Send Custom Offers, up to $10,000 • Priority Customer Support • Eligibility to be featured at promotional listings • Eligibility for Customer Success program • Earning clearance: 14 days
Top Rated	• 30 Active Gigs • 6 Gig Extras ($5, $10, $20, $40, $50, $100) • 20 Gig Multiples • Send Custom Offers, up to $10,000 • VIP Customer Support • Eligibility to be featured at promotional listings • Eligibility for Customer Success program • Earning clearance: 7 days

To see Fiverr's complete Glossary of Terms, visit https://sellers.Fiverr.com/en/article/glossary-of-terms.

There are thousands of freelancers offering millions of Gigs on Fiverr.com. To succeed, you must find ways to stand out from the crowd in a busy marketplace.

Just like a shop in a physical location, you will want your online shop to provide an experience that resonates with your customers. You must capture buyers' attention with your display. Your online shop is your marketing tool. It is where people judge you and your offer. It is where they decide whether to click that Order button or not.

2.2 Setting up your account

Make sure you read, understand and agree to Fiverr's Terms of Service (https://www.fiverr.com/terms_of_service) before joining. You will have to operate within the website's terms or risk losing your account.

Select your username carefully because you cannot change it after you register and activate the account. It helps with your branding when you choose a name that reflects your business. For my PDF form design business, I chose PDFHelper (https://www.fiverr.com/PDFHelper).

2.3 Setting up your profile

A great profile inspires confidence and enthusiasm. It should showcase who you are, why you do what you do, and the principles that guide your work.

Complete your profile professionally and as fully as possible by using the available tools such as videos, photos, images, tags or keywords, and social network links. Make sure you use error-free text and high-quality photos that you own or are entitled to use.

Potential clients want to know that you are credible and able to provide what they need or solve their problem. They will do business with you if they think you are trustworthy.

Craft your profile to display exactly who you are and what makes you unique. Demonstrate why you are the best choice. For example, if you're a designer, show your awesome and visually intriguing profile picture. If you're a writer, make sure your description is engaging and well written.

Take a look at other profiles and Gigs to get inspiration for yours.

In my profile, I wanted to capture the essence of who I am and what I do in a few sentences. I wanted to convey that I am a giving person, passionate and experienced in my field, and I use modern, uncomplicated technologies in the products I produce. Do you think the description below demonstrate my points?

> *I love to create, have been designing forms for years and I am constantly learning new and better techniques. I am on Fiverr.com to help people and companies with their PDF forms and documents. I believe in paying it forward, simple is beautiful and the best things in life are not necessarily expensive.*

2.4 Setting up your Gigs

When you are setting up your individual Gigs, pick the right category and use proper keywords to help buyers to find them. To improve your search ranking, use consistent keywords in your Gig title, description, and tags.

Also think beyond what you are offering, and when possible, present it as a benefit or solution instead of a feature or a task. For example: "I will be like your in-house writer, taking care of all your writing needs." instead of "I will write articles for your website."

Make sure to clearly communicate what the client will get and your expectations. Provide details to help them select you for the job. Make them believe in you, your idea, your product or service. Make them believe they will benefit from it. Here's an example for one of my Gigs:

> *Properly-designed Adobe PDF fillable forms save you money, support your operation, and enhance your customer service. With thoughtful layout and built-in validation, they help your business collect the right information at the front-end to reduce back-end processing.*
>
> *I can design simple static to complex, fully dynamic PDF forms for you to email, print, or put on your website. For this Gig, I will design from scratch (not just simply convert your form unless you wish to do so) a simple form in Adobe Acrobat or Adobe LiveCycle which can include your logo and up to 10 fields. For every additional set of up to 10 fields, please add $5. Fields can include text fields, check boxes, radio buttons, text boxes, buttons (including email submit button).*
>
> *You can use your form with the free Adobe Acrobat Reader.*
>
> *Please send me your form with any instructions and information that would help the construction of your form. It is important to me that the form I design for*

you fully meets your requirements so collaboration is both necessary and appreciated. Thank you!

The number of Gigs increases the chances for buyers to find you, but don't create different versions of the same Gig. When you do that, your customers' ratings and reviews will be scattered and it will take longer to build up an impressive Gig.

You can create multiple unrelated Gigs, for example, copywriting, logo design, and virtual assistant services. But, if you want to build your reputation as an expert in your specialized field, you will want to create related and focused Gigs. Pick one field that you are passionate about that you believe has the best chance to succeed. Focus on building your brand identity and the type of projects you take on. Group them in a way that makes it easy to see what goes well together from a shopper's perspective. For example, if you want to be known as a logo designer then you should only showcase logo projects in your portfolio.

With my technical background, I could offer services such as web design, remote technical support, or web software installation. But, since I wanted to be perceived as an expert in PDFs, all my Gigs are for creating, editing and selling PDF forms and documents. I chose this because I love to design and I know it is a big and unsaturated market where I would excel with my skills and experience.

2.5 Pricing your Gigs

There are different ways to set your prices:

Hourly Rate: Add up all your ongoing monthly expenses (e.g. rent, food, utilities) plus 30% for occasional expenses (e.g. taxes, insurance, vacation) and divide the total into the number of hours you plan to work each month. For example, if your ongoing monthly expenses is $2,000 and your occasional expenses is $600, the total is $2,600. If you plan to work 150 hours per month, your hourly rate will be $17.33 ($2,600 / 150 hours). Based on this hourly rate, you would set your price to $35 for something that takes two hours to do.

Market Rate: Use other freelancers' rates in your field as a guide and adjust your price up or down according to how much you offer in comparison. Since there are freelancers who live in countries with cheaper living expenses, you may find yourself with tougher competition on price.

Value-Driven Rate: Base your fee on the value of the piece to your clients rather than what it costs to produce. Successful freelancers get paid top dollar by getting their clients to understand the value of their expertise and the work they perform. In section 2.8, we will discuss in detail on how to apply value-driven rates.

When you're just getting started with freelancing, your rate should be high enough to put you in the right mindset to deliver exemplary service. On the other hand, you may need to be willing to negotiate in order to gain initial business. You may increase your rate as your client base grows and as you become more experienced. When I first started, I charged $5 to design a simple form because I wanted to gain new business to build my portfolio. Now, even at $30 for similar forms, I know my clients are getting the best possible value on the market.

Before setting up your shop, use the following checklists to identify and gather the information you need.

2.6 Checklist: Items I need to set up my account and profile

Mandatory

☐ Email address _____ or connect through Facebook _____ or Google account _____.

- ☐ Username _____.
- ☐ Password. Password must contain at least eight characters, one uppercase letter, and one number.
- ☐ PayPal email address _____ to associate with the account to receive payments.

Optional

- ☐ Number of working hours desired ____.
- ☐ Income desired _____.
- ☐ Facebook account to link to _____.
- ☐ Google account to link to _____.
- ☐ Dribbble account to link to _____.
- ☐ Stack Overflow account to link to _____.
- ☐ LinkedIn account to link to _____.
- ☐ Languages spoken and fluency _____.
- ☐ Skills:
    1. Skill _____, Experience Level _____.
    2. Skill _____, Experience Level _____.

3. Skill _____, Experience Level _____.

☐ Education:

Country _____.

College/University Name _____.

Title _____.

Degree _____.

Year of Graduation _____.

☐ Certification:

1. Type _____, From _____, Year _____.
2. Type _____, From _____, Year _____.
3. Type _____, From _____, Year _____.

☐ Link to blog or portfolio websites _____.

☐ A self-image photo.

☐ A brief introduction _____.

Downloadable Item
2.6 Checklist: Items I need to set up my account and profile **Log in:** https://goo.gl/MXjBmM or **Sign up:** https://goo.gl/xpPbNM

2.7 Checklist: Items I need to set up my Gig

- ☐ A clear and concise Gig title up to 80 characters _____. Fiverr allows one fully capitalized word per Gig title so you can use that word to highlight the most unique aspect of your Gig.
  - ☐ Category _____ and subcategory for the Gig _____. A service type _____ may be needed for certain category (https://sellers.Fiverr.com/en/article/service-types-faq.)
  - ☐ Up to five search terms _____.
  - ☐ Name of the Gig being offered _____.
  - ☐ Delivery time _____ (days) to complete the Gig.
  - ☐ Items to be included _____.
  - ☐ Number of revisions included in the Gig _____.
  - ☐ Price _____.
  - ☐ Gig extras (optional):
    1. Title _____, Description _____, Amount _____, Delivery time _____.

2. Title _____, Description _____, Amount _____, Delivery time _____.
3. Title _____, Description _____, Amount _____, Delivery time _____.

☐ Shipping & Handling (for non-digital items) (optional):

1. Amount _____ to Country _____.
2. Amount _____ to Country _____.
3. Amount _____ to Country _____.

☐ Description for the Gig (up to 1,200 characters) _____.

☐ Add frequently asked questions (FAQs) and answers to save time (optional).

1. Question 1 _____ Answer 1 _____
2. Question 2 _____ Answer 2 _____
3. Question 3 _____ Answer 3 _____

☐ Requirements for buyer to follow or provide:

1. Requirement _____ Mandatory _____.
2. Requirement _____ Mandatory _____.
3. Requirement _____ Mandatory _____.

- ☐ Up to three images (in jpeg, png or bmp format and up to 50 MB) that describe or relate to the Gig. Be sure you own the rights to the images, or have obtained the proper licenses.
- ☐ A short (30 to 75 seconds and up to 50 MB) video in MP4 or AVI format that describes or relates to the Gig. Video can't include website address or contact information. Fiverr recommends that you mention your Gig is exclusively sold on Fiverr. The status of an active Gig that contains a video will be pending until the video is reviewed and approved by Fiverr (optional but recommended).
- ☐ Up to two PDF files that describe or relate to the Gig (optional).

Downloadable Item
2.7 Checklist: Items I need to set up my Gig **Log in:** https://goo.gl/MXjBmM or **Sign up:** https://goo.gl/xpPbNM

STEP 2: GETTING ORDERS

Once you have your shop set up, it is visible to potential buyers through the website's recommendation system and its search engine.

When your Gig is found, a buyer can either place an order immediately or place an order after communicating with you. Either way, you need to get accurate requirements and set clear expectations for each order so that both sides' needs are satisfied. Although orders are not written using legal terminology, they are contracts between you and your clients.

Ask the buyer to provide requirements in the formats that help you understand them. For example, typed notes in word processing or spreadsheet format, scanned sketches, images, videos, voice recordings.

Fiverr uses response rate to track your first response to a new request. Since response rate is one of the criteria for determining seller level, you need to acknowledge these messages within 24 hours. Reporting spam and solicitations will count as your response to these messages.

This flowchart shows the order handling process after you set up your shop in STEP 1:

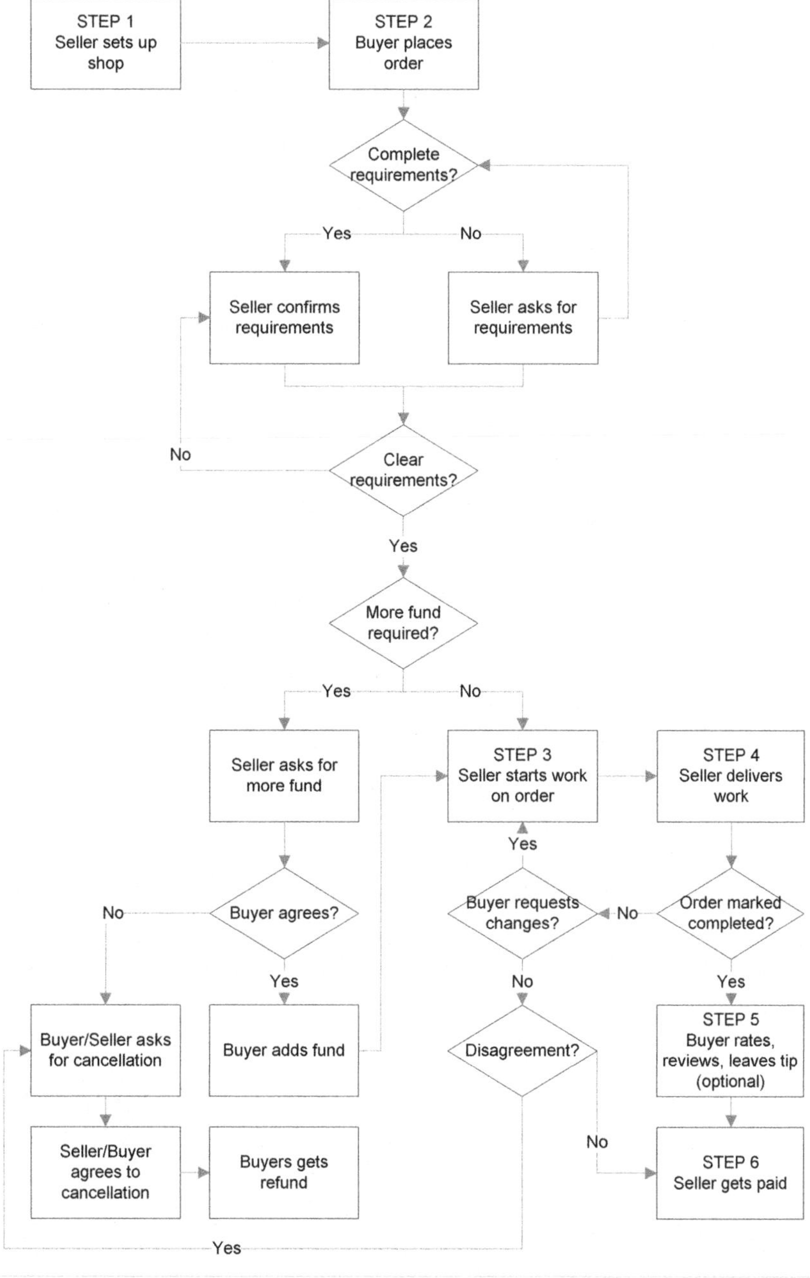

STEP 2

Buyer places an order. The buyer may or may not send you their requirements at this point.

- You either ask for requirements if they are not present or you confirm whether they are complete. To save time, provide the buyer with a list of common questions or items you need, if you have one.
- You ask for clarification if the requirements provided are unclear.

STEP 3

You start work on the order or ask for more money if required.

- The buyer adds more funds if he/she agrees. Otherwise, either you or the buyer can request a cancellation. If the receiving party doesn't reply to the request, the order will be automatically cancelled after two days. Both sides can see the status and have the option to abort the cancellation. The buyer gets his/her refund when the order is cancelled.

STEP 4

You deliver the work and the buyer may request modifications. If there is any disagreement, both sides can request a cancellation.

STEP 5

The buyer has the option to mark the order complete by rating, writing a review, and leaving a tip for the order. If he/she doesn't, the system marks the order completed after three days.

STEP 6

You get paid for the order after a clearing period of up to fourteen days.

2.8 Providing quotes

Depending on what you are offering, there may be times that potential buyers request quotes for custom products or services.

When you provide quotes, show potential clients the value of your service. View your work through your client's eyes and from a commercial perspective. Price your service according to the client and how your work would benefit him/her and affect his/her bottom line. For example, instead of providing just the cost or mention how many hours it takes to write a 1,000-word sales copy, include all the tasks that you will do: such as research, dig through analytics, gather testimonials for proof, write a rough draft, present for evaluation, and revise. Also, think about your market. The price to write an article for a small business blog is going to be less than if you're writing for a large multinational corporation.

Explain to the clients how your process works. Show your interest in them and their business, and then break down your process step-by-step. This helps build trust and confidence, and can be what seals the deal in a proposed project.

When possible, include samples of your work with your quote to show what you're capable of and how your potential client could put your skills to work for as part of his/her team.

Fiverr offers a feature called Custom Offers that allows sellers the flexibility in accommodating personalized requests. As I develop customized forms and documents, I often use this feature to provide tailored solution and pricing to my clients. Custom Offers can be created from any inbox message or in responding to a Customer Request from a buyer.

2.9 The C.O.S.T. model

When I provide quotes, I use my **C.O.S.T.** model that takes the various factors into consideration: Communication, Other, Stakeholders, and Time. I also put an expiration date on the offer to help clients make quicker decisions and to ensure the quote stays current.

- **C**ommunication: The way the client expresses his/her expectations and delivers requirements. This includes time and effort in exchanging or explaining information
- **O**ther: Any other special tools/equipment, considerations, requests (for example, fast delivery), or extra costs/fees incurred.
- **S**takeholders: Whether the client is new or a repeat buyer acting as him/herself or on behalf of someone else.
- **T**ime: The length of time needed for the task or project according to its complexity. Including time doing the work, researching, reviewing, and analyzing requirements.

Sample quote using the C.O.S.T. model

Scenario: Providing a quote for an existing client for a complex project that requires special software.

		Amount
C	The client delivered a comprehensive set of requirements; however, extra effort and time is required to organize them due to the complexity.	$200
O	Special software is required.	$300
S	Discount 10% for being a reasonable repeat customer in the past.	-$150
T	Include extra time to acquire software and analyzing requirements.	$1,000
Total Quote Amount		**$1,350**

2.10 Promoting your Gigs

Fiverr.com provides different tools for buyers to find you. Often buyers use its search and filter functions to find what they need. If you want to, you can do one or more of the following to get more traffic to your service:

- Share your profile and activities on social media.
- Tell people you know about your service.

- Contact past clients.
- Post your service in the forum (https://forum.fiverr.com). When you do, make sure you don't come across as a spammer desperate for business.
- Send Custom Offers using Fiverr Anywhere (https://sellers.Fiverr.com/en/article/using-Fiverr-anywhere-for-sending-custom-offers). This feature allows sellers to customize an offer by posting the generated code on blog, Facebook, messages, etc.
- Reply to Buyer Requests (https://sellers.Fiverr.com/en/article/responding-to-buyer-requests). This feature allows buyers to post a service they are looking for and sellers can send offers to. It's a way for buyers to get propositions from different sellers, and for sellers to get work. This is not a place for sellers to advertise their services.
- Use pay-per-click advertisements such as Facebook Ads and Google AdWords where you pay a fee each time one of your ads is clicked which sends the visitor to your profile or Gig page.

- Build your own website to promote your service. Include client case studies, showcase your work and tell stories about the process behind what you do.

STEP 3: WORKING ON ORDERS

The clock starts once an order is placed. You will need to deliver the work within the timeline promised in your Gig. When you are unable to deliver an order, it will lead to cancellation or a bad review. You may lose your seller level and future prospects.

It is vital that you consistently deliver quality work on time. When your schedule is too tight or too full, your performance will be affected as you get anxious and stressed out. Adjust either your delivery time or the number or type of projects you accept in order to maintain a balanced workload. You can temporarily pause the gig to give yourself time to catch up. You can also delegate or outsource some tasks. Telling clients that you're too busy to take their project right now may make you more desirable to them. This may also be a good opportunity to discuss a retainer arrangement where they'll pay you to work on a regular basis. To help determine if you should take on a project, ask yourself if you have the capability, obligation, and time to do the work.

Have a backup plan in place for occasions when you are unable to work due to emergencies, sickness or equipment breakdown.

Don't accept an order or start work until you are clear about what the client expects. While working on the order, you may need to ask for clarification.

Always make sure that you have the proper tools for the job, that you keep the client's proprietary information confidential, and that the work you produce is not plagiarized. Consult Fiverr's summarized general copyright principles and intellectual property rights at https://sellers.fiverr.com/en/article/copyright-and-intellectual-property-rights.

I often share my work process and thought process with my clients. This helps put them at ease, inform them of the steps I will take, and gives them ideas on how to better their business by using my service.

A good rapport with clients will also make it easier when you need something. In 2014, my younger brother fell sick unexpectedly and passed away. It was a difficult year for our family. In addition to working full-time, being a mother and wife, and travelling back and forth to be with my brother in his final days, I was able to manage my Fiverr business. This was possible because my Fiverr's clients were empathetic after I explained my situation and asked for extra delivery time. Everyone showed their understanding, some sent their prayers and a few shared their own experiences with me. I learned that people respond well to honest and sincere communication. Next time when you need something, explain it clearly and ask politely and you will receive.

STEP 4: DELIVERING WORK

Once you've completed an order, you will need to deliver your work to the buyer. The buyer will review your work, and mark it as complete.

Depending on how you set up your service, you may allow a number of modifications or not. Even if you don't, be prepared to respond to requests to modify work.

When delivering work, in addition to the actual product, you can:

- Include relevant instructions

- Include bonus materials
- Ask for reviews (please don't ask for a particular rating)
- Ask for referrals
- Ask for a tip or a bonus (Fiverr has this tip feature for buyer to leave tip. Be aware that some buyers may not like to be asked.)

If you miss the expected time to deliver, the order will be marked as late and the buyer will be entitled to cancel his/her order if there's no further response from you. If you deliver within 24 hours after the order is marked as late, the buyer will be given the chance to request revisions or complete the order and to rate his/her experience accordingly. If you don't do anything, the buyer will be able to cancel the order from the order page and you will be given an automatic negative rating. Late delivery leaves your client unsatisfied. Negative ratings damage your reputation on Fiverr and affect your seller level status.

Delivering quality products and services is important. How you deliver them is equally important. Treat your clients like gold by providing them with an amazing customer experience. Always strive to deliver more than expected. All of us appreciate the little things.

When you go an extra mile for your clients, you gain their appreciation, great reviews and referrals.

STEP 5: GETTING RATINGS, REVIEWS, AND TIPS

Buyers on Fiverr.com have the option to provide feedback on their overall customer experience by rating, commenting, and leaving tips on each order. Feedback consists of three service levels. Each is rated between one and five stars:

- Communication with Seller
- Service as Described
- Buy Again or Recommend the Seller.

Each time you complete an order and the client is satisfied, ask him/her to rate and write a review about the timeliness and quality of your work. The review will become part of your portfolio and future clients will find it much easier to trust you knowing that someone who's worked with you is happy with the results. Take the opportunity to comment on the feedback. It is a way to promote your service and display your professionalism.

Generally, people like what other people like and reviews are indicators for quality. Positive reviews and references from your existing clients help bring new business.

About 70% of my clients rate and review their experience with me. I have received over 1,000 five-star reviews. Clients can recognize the value and quality I provide from the reviews I received.

When I complete an order, I always let my client know that I appreciate his/her business and that I am there for him/her. Sometimes I request that he/she rate and review the order. I seldom ask but have received tips ranging from $5 to $100 for many orders. Some of the tips I received were for helping people who didn't place an order but had questions or issues. By giving them the instructions or pointing them the direction they needed, more often than not, I'd receive their gratitude, a tip, future business, or all three.

If you receive a negative feedback, you can send a message asking the client to consider changing the feedback, respond to the feedback with your polite and respectful comment explaining your side of the story, or request a feedback revision through the Resolution Center (https://sellers.Fiverr.com/en/article/using-the-resolution-center). Repeatedly requesting feedback revisions may cause your account to be blocked.

Downloadable Item
BONUS GUIDE *The ART of Getting and Responding to Customer Reviews on Fiverr* **Log in:** https://goo.gl/MXjBmM or **Sign up:** https://goo.gl/xpPbNM

STEP 6: GETTING PAID

As soon as an order is marked completed by the buyer or by the system, your account will be credited with 80% of the total order value, including any tip you receive. After a clearing period of up to fourteen days (or seven days for Top Rated Sellers), you can transfer it to your PayPal account, your local bank, Direct Deposit (available in the U.S.), or to a Fiverr Revenue Card that allows users to load their Fiverr earnings and then use it as a regular MasterCard card. You cannot have the Fiverr Revenue Card and Direct Deposit simultaneously.

When you withdraw revenue to your PayPal account, there is a PayPal fee of 2% of the sum withdrawal amount up to $1. Up to $3 is charged for other withdrawal methods. This article provides more information about withdrawals: https://sellers.fiverr.com/en/article/withdrawing-funds.

Consider these fees as the cost of running a business. Fiverr's fees are fixed, but you can minimize withdrawal fees by increasing the withdrawal amount or by reducing the number of withdrawals.

CANCELLATIONS

You should avoid cancellations as they affect your seller status. But, there will be times that you need or want to cancel an order, sometimes after you've started working on it or even after you've delivered the work. The numbers in the brackets after the items below indicate the sections of this book where you can find message templates to use in that situation. Some of the reasons are:

- You and the buyer can't agree on the price or conditions. (4.34)
- You are not able to do the job. (4.7 and 4.8)
- You are not able to complete the order in time. (4.38)
- You didn't receive enough information from the buyer. (4.37)
- You didn't receive enough money for the job. (4.35)
- The buyer requested work that is not offered in your Gig. (4.36)

- The buyer asks for unethical or illegal work. You can report this when you feel it is warranted. (4.36)
- The buyer is not responding. (4.33)
- The buyer orders by mistake. (4.39)
- The buyer changes his/her mind. (4.39)
- The buyer complains or is unhappy. (4.40)
- The buyer is being unreasonable or difficult. (4.40)
- The buyer places duplicate orders due to system glitches. (4.41)
- The buyer places a new order to replace another one. (4.41)

Orders cannot be partially cancelled or refunded. Once an order is created and there is a need to partially cancel/refund the buyer, you can ask the buyer to place a new order and after it is created, cancel the original order.

An order can also be cancelled when a buyer files a dispute with PayPal or has issues with his/her PayPal account. This can happen even after you have been paid through Fiverr. When this happens, Fiverr will terminate the buyer's account and reverse the credit on your account.

Contact the Resolution Center if the buyer refuses your request to cancel the order. You will get better support and resolution when you provide your explanation with proper documentation instead of a complaint or a rant.

When you open your door for business, expect to deal with anyone coming through. Freelance work involves working with all kinds of customers. Section 5.2 gives suggestions on how to handle different types of clients.

My clients came from different places and mindsets and it's not possible to please everyone. While most of the people I dealt with were nice and reasonable, some were controlling, difficult, or unreasonable. There will be those who find reasons not to pay after work is delivered. Every time I get an unreasonable, difficult, or confused client, I challenge myself to remain patient and understanding. So far this has resulted in many repeat clients. A calm and professional demeanor goes a long way in building great business relationships and repeat business.

As you become more experienced, you will be able to vet new clients. Focus on spending your time, effort and energy with clients that understand and appreciate your value. You can't build your reputation with clients that are impossible to work with, so it is better to wish them luck and let them go. Also let go of projects you are not equipped to do, you are uncomfortable doing, or you don't believe they align with your goals and values.

SUPPORT & TOOLS

When you're first starting out, it can be incredibly daunting and you may feel that you are struggling on your own. Participate in forum discussions (https://forum.fiverr.com) to get advice and support from others. Know that you are not alone and if you need help from Fiverr.com, support is just a click away (https://support.fiverr.com).

Fiverr.com constantly upgrades its platform to provide new tools and functions. Use them to help you be more efficient and organized. Some of the useful tools are:

- **FAQs**: Use the Frequently Asked Questions section in each Gig to provide answers to common issues and concerns. Think about what your buyer would want to know about the Gig and create a good response that shows you understand his/her needs.

- **Quick Responses:** Save clips of text as Quick Responses so you can insert them quickly in your messages. Use this method to record some of the frequently-used messages that you find in the **Sample Scenarios & Message Templates** chapter in this book.
- **Limit Orders in Queue:** Manage your workload by setting a limit on the number of orders you want to receive. Once the limit you set is reached, your Gig will be paused.
- **Vacation Mode:** Let buyers know that you're away and when you'll return.
- **Sales Analytics:** System displays statistics in regarding your sales, activities, etc.
- **Gig Statistics:** System displays an overview of your Gig's performance.

BEING A SUCCESSFUL FREELANCER

As you can see, almost anyone with a set of core or technical skills can start his/her freelancing business. But for every freelancer who earns a 6-figure income, there are thousands of those who earn little or nothing. Becoming a successful freelancer requires additional soft or transferrable skills. Success in this context is defined by getting paid one's worth and having the freedom to choose clients or projects.

Core or technical skills (also known as hard skills) are skills such as computer, administrative, or bookkeeping skills. Soft skills or transferable skills include those such as leadership skills, conflict resolution skills, or problem-solving abilities.

In this chapter, we will discuss ways to keep your core skills current. We will also examine the three must-have soft skills: Communication, negotiation, and time management. Take the following self-assessment to see what you already have and what you need to work on.

3.1 Self-Assessment: Do I have what it takes?

- ☐ I have a clear purpose, defined goals, and realistic expectations for my freelancing business.
- ☐ I am able to see where I am heading and can rise above the hard and boring days.
- ☐ I can operate without immediate or positive feedback.
- ☐ I am willing to be flexible to accommodate my client's needs. I can say 'No' when necessary.
- ☐ I have a positive attitude.
- ☐ I am genuinely interested in my client's success.
- ☐ I have a sense of humour.
- ☐ I am reliable.
- ☐ I take calculated risks.

- ☐ I take time to reflect on my methods, my delivery, and the way I connect with my clients.
- ☐ I commit to building relationships and connections.
- ☐ I am good at what I do and I enjoy my work.
- ☐ I know the value I bring to my clients.
- ☐ I am comfortable with the unknowns and I welcome change.
- ☐ I am curious. I never stop learning. I take time to learn new, useful, and relevant tools or skills.
- ☐ I am able to research to find answers to problems I don't know how to solve.
- ☐ I communicate and negotiate with clients effectively and productively.
- ☐ I view other freelancers as potential collaborators, not competitors. I network, share experience, and make referrals.

☐ I practise self-care. I avoid isolation and overwork. I take time off to relax and de-stress as necessary.

☐ I have a reward system that will allow me to set the bar high and push myself.

☐ I plan and prioritize my work to stay ahead of my responsibilities, keep deadlines, and produce the best quality for my work.

Downloadable Item
3.1 Self-Assessment: Do I have what it takes? **Log in:** https://goo.gl/MXjBmM or **Sign up:** https://goo.gl/xpPbNM

The list may seem overwhelming. Don't give up freelancing because you didn't check off every item on it. You do not need to have all these attributes and competencies right at the moment, but you do need to acquire them over time through awareness, education, and experience.

CORE SKILLS

Aside from learning business skills, you must keep your core skills current to help you stay competitive and relevant. Commit to continue learning and practising your skills daily. Learning a new skill is also important as it can open new opportunities for you while improving your abilities and boosting your confidence. Amazing things happen when you are open to new ideas, scenarios, and experiences.

Find out what skills and qualifications would give you an edge in your field. Identify your strengths and weaknesses then do everything possible to make yourself more proficient so that you can always deliver your best quality work on time.

Whether you are experienced or not, your job is to perform better than everyone else in your field, both in the work you do, and the way you act.

3.2 Ways to upgrade your core skills

- Read blogs, books, magazines and journals.
- Take in-person or online classes.
- Attend conferences, trade shows, workshops, and mentoring programs.
- Watch videos, podcasts, and webinars.
- Local small business support organizations and associations.
- Search the Internet.

- Participate in forum discussions.
- Email, call and follow the experts in your field.
- Read blogs and sign up for newsletters and RSS feeds.
- Volunteer to acquire skills and gain relevant experience.

3.3 List of learning websites and apps

There are many high quality educational websites and apps that provide resources on various subjects, some are completely free:

- **Alison** https://alison.com – Free knowledge and workplace skills training.
- **Anki** https://apps.ankiweb.net – A free flashcard program which makes remembering things easy.
- **Babbel** https://www.babbel.com –Free language lessons with integrated speech recognition.
- **Brain Pump** http://brainpump.net – Free educational videos on various topics.
- **Busuu** https://www.busuu.com – Free and premium language courses.
- **Code.org** https://code.org – Free computer science, biology, chemistry, and algebra courses.

- **Codecademy** https://www.codecademy.com – Free and premium courses on JavaScript, HTML, CSS, Python, Java, SQL, Bash/Shell, and Ruby.
- **CodeCombat** https://codecombat.com – A free platform for students to learn computer science while playing through a real game.
- **Coffeestrap** http://www.coffeestrap.com – Free language learning platform through real conversations with people that have the same interests.
- **Coursera** https://www.coursera.org – Paid online courses from top universities and organizations.
- **Curiosity** https://curiosity.com – Free learning on interesting topics.
- **DataCamp** https://www.datacamp.com – Free and premium courses on R, Python and data visualisation.
- **Duolingo** https://www.duolingo.com – Free language courses in over 20 different languages.
- **Free Code Camp** https://www.freecodecamp.org – Free courses on HTML5, CSS3, JavaScript, Databases, Git & GitHub, Node.js, React.js, and D3.js.

- **High Brow** https://gohighbrow.com – Free 10-day courses with 5-minute lessons that are delivered by daily email.
- **InstaNerd** http://instanerd.me – Provides endless stream of random facts and how-to's.
- **Instructables** http://www.instructables.com – Free place to explore, learn, document, and share your creations.
- **Khan Academy** https://www.khanacademy.org – Free courses in math, science, computer programming, history, art history, economics, and more.
- **Lingvist** https://lingvist.com – A learning tool to help you learn language effectively and efficiently.
- **Lrnapp** http://lrnapp.com – A free app which provides interactive mini-quizzes to help learn HTML, CSS, Python, Ruby, and JavaScript.
- **Make:** https://makezine.com – Free guides on how to make things.

- **Memrise** https://www.memrise.com – Over 200 free and premium courses in a variety of subjects via digital flashcards and crowdsourced mnemonics.
- **Pianu** https://pianu.com – Free piano-learning website where you can play interactively.
- **Snapguide** https://snapguide.com – Free iOS app and web service for those that want to create and share step-by-step "how to guides" on a wide array of topics including cooking, gardening, crafts, repairs, do-it-yourself projects, fashion tips, entertaining and more.
- **TedEd** https://ed.ted.com/lessons – Free curated educational videos on various topics.
- **Udemy** https://www.udemy.com – Over 55,000 free and premium courses taught by expert instructors on various topics including technology, photography and business skills.
- **Yousician** http://yousician.com – Offers paid plans for learning guitar, bass, piano, and ukelele.

COMMUNICATION SKILLS

As a freelancer, your income depends on how you communicate. Corresponding with clients, dealing with difficult buyers, resolving disputes, handling cancellations, and managing delays are part of your daily life as a freelancer. You will rely mainly on electronic direct one-on-one communication such as email. Because you cannot use the nonverbal cues and vocal inflections common in face-to-face communication, you must be particularly careful to communicate clearly and effectively. It is easy to get stuck in a time-wasting never-ending email chain. Sometimes message exchanges stop suddenly without any indication. In-person conversations allow you to get feedback through spoken words or through body language. Email exchanges offer no such luxury. You must develop the ability to assess comprehension, confidence, interest, engagement, and truthfulness without nonverbal cues.

To be a successful freelancer, you must know how to communicate your ideas clearly and understand the information conveyed to you. You must also understand your client's emotions and underlying feelings. Your ability to communicate clearly, concisely and effectively will save time and minimize confusion for you and your clients. All communication needs to aim toward producing results.

Communication skills must be learned and practised. It is normal to struggle with putting ideas and thoughts on paper or in an email. Developing your communication skills is as much about improving the quality of your relationships as it is about expressing yourself.

Since you often don't get a second chance to make your point in a different way, you need to present your points in a style, manner, and sequence that suits the message you are sending. Think before composing your messages. Choose your words carefully to minimize misunderstandings and conflicts.

3.4 Self-Assessment: Am I a good communicator?

Select all the statements that apply to you:

☐ I am conscious of my tone, attitude, nuance, and other subtleties my message may convey. I take the time to clarify my message.

☐ When I am upset or angry I allow myself time to calm down before responding.

- ☐ I try to appreciate other people's points of view.
- ☐ I can show attentiveness and understanding of what's being said.
- ☐ I can listen actively, for example, deferring judgement until I've heard everything that the other person has to say.
- ☐ I don't make assumptions.
- ☐ I choose my words carefully.
- ☐ I take time to understand my client and think about how best to approach him/her.
- ☐ I ask appropriate questions to get the information I need.
- ☐ I listen intelligently to what my client needs and expectations.
- ☐ I consider not only what I'll say, but also how I think my client will perceive it.
- ☐ I compose my message with a purpose and know what I want my message to achieve.

- ☐ I avoid using acronyms and jargon. I keep my message simple.
- ☐ I organize information to make my message easy to follow and understand.
- ☐ I try to anticipate and predict possible causes of confusion, and deal with them up front.
- ☐ I consider cultural and language barriers.
- ☐ I am tactful.

Downloadable Item
3.4 Self-Assessment: Am I a good communicator? **Log in:** https://goo.gl/MXjBmM or **Sign up:** https://goo.gl/xpPbNM

3.5 What is tact?

Tact is the ability to deliver a message in a way that respects your own rights and considers your client's feelings. As it is easier to deliver good or positive messages than to deliver bad or negative ones, being tactful is particularly useful in negotiations and when conflicts or difficult situations arise. Tactful communication can relieve tension, remove blame, and allow both sides to save face and preserve a good working relationship.

Tactful communication strengthens your reputation and builds your credibility and relationships. Tact encompasses many things, including self-awareness, compassion, respect, thoughtfulness, empathy, discretion, subtlety, honesty, diplomacy, and courtesy.

When you communicate tactfully, you demonstrate good manners that show your character, maturity, professionalism, and integrity. If you can communicate with grace and consideration, you'll stand out from the crowd, and you'll get noticed for the right reasons. This can lead to more income prospects.

3.6 The BASIC test for written communication

Written communication creates permanent records which can be easily referenced. Your emails and correspondence are ideal for documenting understanding, acceptance, and verifying when issues arise. Everything you write should be of a quality that every reader will find acceptable. Clear written communication minimizes misunderstanding and frustration while building long-term relationships with your clients.

I've developed this **BASIC** test to help you write effective messages so your audience understands what you want to achieve:

- B = Brief
- A = Appropriate
- S = Significant
- I = Intention
- C = Considerate

Before composing your message, determine its purpose or intention. If you don't know what the point of your message is, your audience won't either. Knowing your intention will help you compose your message. Once you know the destiny, you will be able to figure out the different routes to get there. If you can make your audience understand your intention, they are more likely to go there with you. Keep your purpose in mind when you compose your message. For example, is the purpose of your message to inform/educate, collaborate/connect, or negotiate/persuade? If you are replying to a message or request, you will also need to decipher the sender's intention when it is not obvious. Before you start communicating, take a moment to figure out what you want to say, and why. Conveying information that is wrong or unnecessary wastes your time and may confuse your clients.

When you present significant details and facts logically while keeping your message brief and timely, you minimize misinterpretation and make it easier and faster for your audience to read and understand. Include only relevant details that match the intention. Your message is effective when your audience understands you and knows what you want them to do. Provide everything they need to be informed or take action. When you need to help your client make decisions, provide your viewpoints in an unbiased way.

Make sure the message is appropriate for the audience and the occasion. Choose words and phrases that the audience can understand for the purpose intended.

When you take into consideration your audience's opinions, knowledge, mindset, background, feelings, you show them your respect, care, and sincerity. Being considerate helps your communication stay friendly, open, and honest. Use "please" and "thank you" abundantly and always acknowledge people with kindness. Use "would you" instead of "could you" when you ask for something as the subtle difference has a psychological influence that helps the receiving person be more receptive to the request. You want to avoid situations where the other person thinks he/she could but wouldn't do what you ask.

Use the following checklist for your messages to help them pass the BASIC test while writing, editing, and proofreading your words or sentences, keep in mind the overarching questions in each part:

B – Is it needed?

A – Is it appropriate?

S – Can it be understood?

I – Does it serve the purpose?

C – Does it show consideration?

3.7 Checklist: Does my message pass the BASIC test?

Brief - Is it needed?

- ☐ Did I focus on details and facts relevant to my purpose of the message?
- ☐ Did I stick to the point and keep it brief without repeating or rambling?

- ☐ Did I delete unnecessary adjectives, filler words and sentences?
- ☐ Did I minimize the number of ideas in each sentence?

***A**ppropriate – Is it appropriate?*

- ☐ Is the message free from grammatical errors and typos, including spellings of names and titles?
- ☐ Did I remove technical terms that my client may not understand?
- ☐ Did I use proper language at the appropriate level?
- ☐ Is my tone appropriate for the situation?

***S**ignificant – Can it be understood?*

- ☐ Did I provide my client a clear picture of what I am telling him/her, for example, use relevant diagrams, charts, and videos to explain my idea or thought?
- ☐ Did I give my client everything he/she needs to be informed and, if applicable, take action?
- ☐ Is my message logical? For example, is each point I made relevant and connected to the main topic?

☐ Does the flow of my message make sense?

Intention – Does it serve the purpose?

☐ Am I clear about my goal for sending the message?

☐ Do I understand what I need and want to say?

☐ Will my client be able to understand why he/she is reading the message?

☐ Will my client understand the meaning of my message without making any assumptions?

Considerate – Does it show consideration?

☐ Did I focus on positive words and facts?

☐ Did I consider my client's opinions, knowledge, mindset, background, emotion, problem, reaction, concern, or intention?

☐ Did I consider the context or situation?

☐ Did I show compassion and kindness?

Downloadable Item
3.7 Checklist: Does my message pass the BASIC test? **Log in:** https://goo.gl/MXjBmM or **Sign up:** https://goo.gl/xpPbNM

3.8 Scenarios for the BASIC test

Below are three scenarios showing the differences between bad and good messages and how they fail or pass the BASIC test. As you will see, bad communication can end the relationship with the client and prevent sales.

Scenario 1 – Handling a complaint/misunderstanding

You are replying to a potential client when he/she says that your quote doesn't seem to match your advertisement. Your goal is to inform the client of your service and its value.

Bad example:

I don't know why you complain. My ad is very clear and this is my final offer. I have many happy clients. You wanted a lot and you are not willing to pay for than its ok.

Why this message fails the BASIC test:

- It focuses on the ad and places blame on the client. "I have many happy clients" is irrelevant to the purpose of the message.

- The tone is unfriendly. It contains a misused word: "than" instead of "then".
- It does not provide any useful information. The client doesn't know what to do next.
- It does not fulfill the goal of the message. It does not tell the client anything about your service and its value.
- It does not consider the client's opinion.

Good example:

Thank you for your feedback.

My quote is based on my ad for a 1,000-word sales copy which includes researching, writing a rough draft, presenting for your evaluation, and revising it to your requirements. The extra $100 is for analyzing analytics and gathering testimonials for proof, as per your request.

I will start work as soon as I receive your order. Please click the Accept button below before noon this Friday when the offer expires.

I look forward to an opportunity to work with you.

Why this message passes the BASIC test:

- It focuses on the offer and promotes your service.

- It uses proper language. The tone is professional.
- It provides useful information for the client to make a decision and lets him/her know what to do next.
- It fulfills the goal of informing the client about your service and its value.
- It takes the client's opinion into consideration.

Scenario 2 – Resolving a conflict/criticism

You are replying to a paying client when he/she says that you didn't deliver work as agreed. Your goal is to collaborate with the client to build trust.

Bad example:

What do you mean I didn't deliver work as agreed? I worked day and night to make this for you and you are not happy?! What else do you want? Everyone want anything for free!!!

Why this message fails the BASIC test:

- It focuses on you and "Everyone want anything for free" is irrelevant to the purpose of the message.

- It contains grammatical errors, excessive punctuation marks, and defensive tone.
- It does not provide any workable suggestion. The client doesn't know what to do next.
- It does not fulfill the goal of the message. It does not encourage collaboration.
- It does not consider the client's concern or reaction.

Good Example:

> *Thank you for your feedback.*
>
> *We agreed that the end product is a 1,000-word sales copy which I delivered after spending time to research, analyze analytics, gather testimonials for proof, write a rough draft, present for your evaluation, and revise it to your requirements.*
>
> *It is important to me that you get everything we agreed on. Would you please let me know what is missing?*

Why this message passes the BASIC test:

- It focuses on the issue and sets clear responsibilities.
- It uses proper language. The tone is friendly and approachable.

- It provides details that help the client to re-evaluate his/her assessment and it asks him/her to do the next step.
- It fulfills the goal of the message of encouraging collaboration and building trust.
- It addresses the client's concern.

Scenario 3 – Negotiating an agreement

You are replying to an existing client when he/she asks for more work but offers a low amount. Your goal is to persuade the client of your good offer.

Bad example:

Are you joking me? You will get nothing for that amount! I have many clients and not that kind of money. I need more! You don't know how much things cost around here. I work really hard and I don't make enough. Everyone wants the same thing!!! People want more and more things but want to pay less and less. OMG! I am so tired of this. I have a family and I need to feed them you know! Can you pay more please? It's just little more and you can afford it. I really need this job so please! I promise to do a good job for you.

Why this message fails the BASIC test:

- It focuses on money and you. It contains irrelevant and rambling details.
- It contains grammatical errors, excessive punctuation marks, and sounds desperate.
- It does not provide any option. It doesn't give information to help the client to make a decision.
- It does not fulfill the goal of the message. It does not persuade the client of your good offer.
- It does not consider the client's intention or reaction.

Good example:

Thank you for asking.

I wish I could write five 100-word sales copies for $25 as you suggested. For $25, I will write two 100-word sales copies for you. My usual charge for these sales copies is $15 each so you will save $5.

I will start work as soon as I receive your order. Please click the Accept button below before noon this Friday when the offer expires.

I look forward to continuing working with you.

Why this message passes the BASIC test:

- It focuses on the value of your service and provides relevant details to support it.
- It uses proper language. The tone is friendly and professional.
- It gives the client an option and lets him/her know what to do next.
- It fulfills the goal of the message of persuading the client to consider your good offer.
- It considers the client's intention.

Focus on your ultimate goal and know that no matter what you do, you are in a relationship building business. Show consideration and compassion for all clients and potential clients, whether or not they are paying you. Treat every person with respect and take every interaction as a learning opportunity with an open, curious mind, and a positive attitude. Over time, your competency, confidence, and reputation will improve, and so will your income.

Offer your expert advice and knowledge appropriately and generously. You are here to solve your clients' problems and to create mutually beneficial situations. Make yourself a valuable and trusted person your clients can count on. Prove that their money is wisely invested with you. Give them reasons to come back to you because repeat business is good business.

Listen carefully to instructions and be patient in getting the information you need. Do not make assumptions and do not be afraid to ask when you are unsure. When in doubt, always ask. Promptly and gladly fix mistakes, sometimes even those that are not yours.

NEGOTIATION SKILLS

Working out terms, pricing, or design choices is part of a freelancer's work. It's important that you practise and master negotiation skills because your income and your workload depend on it. Many of us fear that negotiation will end in awkward disagreement or total dissolution of the relationship, but good negotiation is simply about communicating expectations. Negotiation is an ongoing process. Successful negotiation requires effective communication and goodwill. Your offer needs to be realistic or you'll lose credibility and opportunities.

Negotiations are about building a relationship where both sides are happy. Everyone wins when they trust, respect, understand,

and enjoy working together. You will gain much more when you start negotiation from the standpoint of interests. Interests are the *reasons* behind *what* you want. For example, when you ask a client for more time or money for a project, *what* you want is time or money. The *reason* is because you want to provide the best possible product or solution for your client so that you can build trust and gain his/her testimonial for future business. In other words, it's much more effective when you negotiate with "I want to provide you the best possible service" than "I want you to give me more money." Offer workable options or solutions and be willing to find ways for both sides to get their interests met. Use statements such as "What if we tried this?", "What do you think about this?", or "How about this?"

When you present options to clients as part of the negotiation, offer two and no more than four options. For each option or solution, explain pros and cons and emphasize the benefits that the client will gain.

Negotiation involves two parties working to resolve a problem. The problem cannot be solved to everyone's satisfaction unless everyone understands it. Both parties should walk away feeling like they will get what they need from the relationship. You also need to know when to walk away without damaging the relationship.

Clients don't always know what needs to happen on your end for their project to become a reality. Therefore, you need to help create value in their minds by educating them on what you'll be building for them. The value of the project goes up when you do this well.

Negotiation happens before and after an order is placed. Buyers may ask to add or change something while you are working on the order, after it is delivered, and sometimes months later (for example, clients ask me to change their business information on their forms because they have moved or changed their logos.) I always accommodate as much as I can but when it is not reasonably possible, I'll provide an explanation and offer the clients the options to add more money or cancel. I learned that providing the option to cancel shows my confidence and makes the client feel in control, which is always a good thing. Don't be afraid to say "no" when you can't do something, don't want to, or don't need the job.

I faced challenges that all freelancers experience: dealing with clients who asked for more than what was agreed, insisted on too many revisions, or didn't want to approve extra time or money. Those types of clients are always there, but since I've learned how to identify, communicate, and negotiate with them, I am able to choose clients I want to work with and set my prices accordingly.

Taking the time to achieve clarity at the beginning will save you time and frustration in the long run. Negotiate early and fairly. If you have any objections, raise them before giving your firm agreement.

Take the following self-assessment to see how you are at negotiating.

3.9 Self-Assessment: How effective am I as a negotiator?

- ☐ I am able to assess and clarify clients' expectations. I understand what the client is really looking for and his/her timeline.
- ☐ I am able to ask appropriate questions.
- ☐ I am able to identify and summarize the issues concisely.
- ☐ I am able to build on common ground and on my clients' ideas.
- ☐ I am able to explain precisely why my offer is reasonable.

- ☐ I am able to emphasize areas of agreement.
- ☐ I am able to use clear and simple language.
- ☐ I am able to express my emotions in a constructive way and keep my emotions in check during the negotiation.
- ☐ I am able to be firm without being aggressive. I am able to state my position and opinions without attacking or ignoring the other side's position and opinions.
- ☐ I am able to express my disagreement without using irritating or provocative language, for example, "That's ridiculous!" or "You've got to be joking!"
- ☐ I am able to act professionally even when the client is not.
- ☐ I am able to seek a variety of mutually beneficial solutions to problems.
- ☐ I have patience and the ability to persuade the client without deceit or manipulation into doing, believing, or purchasing something that has no benefit to him/her.
- ☐ I can maintain a calm demeanor during a difficult negotiation.

- ☐ I am able to deliver on my promise.
- ☐ I am able to state my desired outcome as well as my reasoning.
- ☐ I am able to act decisively during a negotiation.
- ☐ I can keep the conversation focused on the matters being negotiated instead of the other side's personality or other issues not directly relevant to making a deal.
- ☐ I am able to choose my words wisely and carefully because it is very hard to change a written agreement.
- ☐ I know which specific items I want to negotiate.
- ☐ I make sure the client knows the value of the item being negotiated.
- ☐ I make sure that the other side knows that I am serious about working out a deal.
- ☐ I am able to avoid, ignore, or downplay ultimatums of any kind.
- ☐ I know at what point I will walk away.

☐ I am prepared to walk away without an agreement.

☐ I am able focus on the intent of the questions instead of the questions themselves. For example, understand the *why* behind the question.

☐ I am able to separate the important things from the minute ones.

☐ I am able to make up my own mind and not believe everything I am told.

☐ I am able to ask open-ended questions to encourage the client to tell me more.

Downloadable Item
3.9 Self-Assessment: How effective am I as a negotiator? **Log in:** https://goo.gl/MXjBmM or **Sign up:** https://goo.gl/xpPbNM

Use the following checklist to help you to better communicate your expectations.

3.10 Checklist: Making persuasive arguments

☐ Why am I communicating to this person in the first place?

☐ Is this communication necessary?

☐ Am I clear with the purpose of my communication? For example, do I provide information, educate, call for action, persuade, present ideas/analyses, solve problem, or entertain?

☐ What emotion do I want to evoke, for example, fear, trust, loyalty?

☐ What tone will I use, formal or informal?

☐ Do I know what my client's expectations are?

☐ What events are surrounding this communication?

☐ What background information do I need to supply?

☐ What do I need to present to make sure my points are clear?

☐ Are there counterarguments I should bring up and then refute?

☐ Do I need to establish who I am and reveal my biases, beliefs, values and assumptions?

- ☐ Do the client and I have shared values I can draw on?
- ☐ How do my client's beliefs fit with my message?
- ☐ Do I need to explain where my expertise comes from?
- ☐ Do I need to use expert testimony?
- ☐ Do I need to show why I should be considered an authority?
- ☐ Do I know how my client will use the information I provide?
- ☐ Have I presented a logical, well-constructed argument?
- ☐ How do I support my claims?
- ☐ Do I have the supporting evidence?
- ☐ How will I deliver the communication?

Downloadable Item
3.10 Checklist: Making persuasive arguments **Log in:** https://goo.gl/MXjBmM or **Sign up:** https://goo.gl/xpPbNM

Effective negotiation means getting consensus, not necessarily giving in or giving up. When disagreements occur, exercise your judgement in doing what is right for you. Have the courage to accept the consequences.

TIME MANAGEMENT SKILLS

Time management is about using your time more effectively to achieve your goals more quickly and with less stress. It is also about choosing and focusing your time and energy on matters that help your business. It is a skill that takes time to develop. By making constant improvements to the way you think and work, you will get more important work done each day.

3.11 Self-Assessment: How good am I at managing my time?

- ☐ I schedule difficult tasks at the time when I work best.
- ☐ I set clear goals.
- ☐ I keep my schedule current. It includes everything important I need to do.
- ☐ I have a list of important but non-urgent small tasks that can be done anytime.
- ☐ I group and do similar tasks consecutively.
- ☐ I avoid procrastination.

- ☐ I prioritize my tasks to focus on those that are more important.
- ☐ I know whether the tasks I am working on are high, medium, or low value.
- ☐ I have the supplies and tools needed to do my job.
- ☐ I know how to minimize interruptions, such as phone calls and unexpected visits.
- ☐ I separate and schedule my tasks in different lists, for example, work and home.
- ☐ I know how much time I spend on each of my tasks.
- ☐ I set realistic deadlines and stick to them.
- ☐ I leave contingency time in my schedule to deal with unexpected events.
- ☐ I focus and concentrate on one thing instead of multitasking.
- ☐ I keep accurate records.
- ☐ I organize my workplace so I can find things easily.

☐ I set aside time for planning and scheduling.

☐ I have patience and take the allotted time required to do a job properly instead of rushing and making mistakes.

☐ I know when not to accept additional tasks/projects and can politely refuse them.

☐ I know when I am not the right person to perform the task/project.

☐ I prioritize by eliminating low-priority tasks.

☐ I use technology to automate tasks when possible.

☐ I delegate tasks when necessary.

☐ I can foresee the steps required to complete a project and how they fit together.

☐ When errors occur, I am able to find the issue quickly and explain the necessary changes clearly.

☐ When setbacks occur, I know how to bounce back quickly and reduce the time lost when things go wrong.

Downloadable Item

3.11 Self-Assessment: How good am I at time management?

Log in: https://goo.gl/MXjBmM or **Sign up:** https://goo.gl/xpPbNM

3.12 How to prioritize your work

Time management requires you to invest time upfront to plan and prioritize. To prioritize your time and your workload, you must understand what is *important* and what is *urgent*.

Important refers to outcome and *Urgent* refers to time. For example, an *important* task brings a positive outcome to your business. An *urgent* task requires your prompt attention or action.

Group your tasks on your work schedule into one of these four types and prioritize them based on the following order. Focus your effort on the top items and defer or eliminate non-essential ones.

1. **Important and Urgent** – A task that matters and needs immediate attention.
2. **Urgent** – A task that needs immediate attention but may or may not matter.

3. **Important but not Urgent** – A task that matters but does not need immediate attention.
4. **Not Important and not Urgent** – A task that does not matter nor needs immediate attention.

This table includes examples of tasks for each group. To increase productivity, it is helpful to set strict timeframes for each activity.

Type	Examples
Important and Urgent	• Delivering work to a client before the deadline in an hour. • Providing a quote right away as you promised.
Urgent	• Responding to a message from a client that you're expecting (matter). • Answering your chat box or telephone before the caller ends the call (may or may not matter).
Important but not Urgent	• Researching a better way to do something. • Reading a client's review of your work.

Type	Examples
Not Important and not Urgent	• Checking social media networks for friends' casual updates. • Responding to a common rant in the forum.

The following is a sample of a daily schedule that you can download to use online or offline. The online PDF version allows you to add, remove, sort, and move lines.

MY DAILY SCHEDULE

1. IMPORTANT AND URGENT - *Tasks that matter and need immediate attention.*	Completed
1	
2	
3	
4	
5	

2. URGENT - *Tasks that needs immediate attention but may or may not matter.*	Completed
1	
2	
3	
4	
5	

3. IMPORTANT BUT NOT URGENT - *Tasks that matter but don't require immediate attention.*	Completed
1	
2	
3	
4	
5	

4. NOT IMPORTANT AND NOT URGENT - *Tasks that don't matter or need immediate attention.*	Completed
1	
2	
3	
4	
5	

Downloadable Item
3.12 My Daily Schedule **Log in:** https://goo.gl/MXjBmM or **Sign up:** https://goo.gl/xpPbNM

To avoid delays and missed deadlines, you will also need to consider and monitor overlapping and dependent tasks. There will be times when one task cannot be started until another task is finished. Your schedule may also require others to complete tasks before you can move forward.

When you are on top of everything and you know exactly what is going on, you can make effective decisions and provide information more quickly. Let's take a self-assessment to see how good you are at organizing your work space.

3.13 Self-Assessment: How good am I at organizing?

☐ I arranged my desk for maximum efficiency, productivity, and comfort.

☐ I put frequently-used items close by.

☐ I have enough space and minimize putting non-work related around me.

- ☐ I keep my supplies together and replenished regularly.
- ☐ I keep my tools in good working order.
- ☐ I use an effective system for reminders.
- ☐ I have effective filing systems for my digital and physical files.
- ☐ I have backups for my files.

Downloadable Item
3.13 Self-Assessment: How good am I at organizing? **Log in:** https://goo.gl/MXjBmM or **Sign up:** https://goo.gl/xpPbNM

Regardless of your subject area, accurate information is essential. You do not have to know everything off the top of your head but you can save time when you know where to find information when you need it. Determine what information you need to have and put systems in place to ensure it is collected and stored. It's better to stay organized than to lose time and be frantic and stressed. Setting up a proper filing system takes time, but once the system is set up, you can store and retrieve information quickly.

For example, to help me store, retrieve, and reference files more quickly, I created a folder structure as shown to keep different types of files. When I get a new client, I copy that _Client Name folder (the underscore in front of the folder name is to allow it to stay on top or bottom when sorted), rename it to the client's username and rename the Order Number folder to match the order number on Fiverr. I also make regular backups of my files by synching them to the cloud so I could access from anywhere and in case my computer crashes.

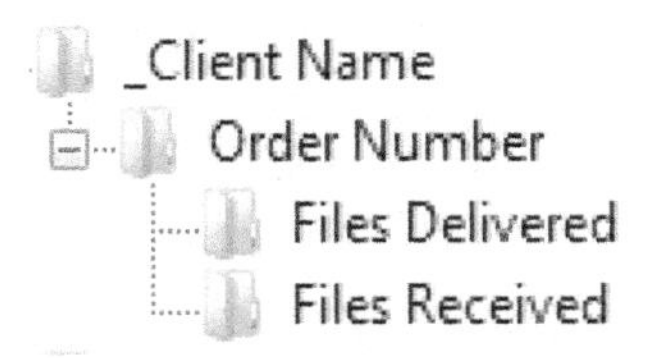

As freelancers, it's easy to overwork to keep clients happy. Furthermore, many freelancers do not maintain enough separation between their business and personal lives. When combined with the constant connections through technological media, we often become overstimulated. It's important to shut down periodically to avoid burn out. Take the self-assessment below to find out how good are you at de-stressing.

3.14 Self-Assessment: How good am I at de-stressing?

- ☐ I take regular 10-15 minute breaks to rejuvenate my body and mind.
- ☐ I get enough rest.
- ☐ I exercise regularly.
- ☐ I set and stick to my maximum number of hours for work each day.
- ☐ I minimize caffeine intake.
- ☐ I keep my interactions with others active.
- ☐ I eat healthy snacks.
- ☐ I set up my workstation properly to ensure safety, efficiency, and comfort.
- ☐ I dress appropriately and comfortably.
- ☐ When things go wrong, I give people the benefit of the doubt because people rarely get things wrong on purpose.

Downloadable Item
3.14 Self-Assessment: How good am I at de-stressing?

Log in: https://goo.gl/MXjBmM or **Sign up:** https://goo.gl/xpPbNM

Do your best to manage your time. But, you must also accept that you won't be able to do everything you set out to do. At times it can be overwhelming and stressful with competing deadlines and priorities. Take a moment to pause and get your life and priorities into perspective. The world will not end if you fail to achieve your last task of the day, or leave it until tomorrow, or stop working early. Tomorrow is another day to get back on track.

A small amount of work pressure helps motivate you to take action and do a good job. Too much pressure will become stress. You may feel you can no longer cope with the demands placed upon you. Stress is not a good thing and it has a negative impact on your health, performance and time management. If you experience stress, you will have so many things on your mind that you will find it practically impossible to focus on the task at hand. As a result, it will take you longer to perform even the simplest of tasks. A backlog will start to build up as you fall behind. Falling behind increases your stress levels and so the spiral continues. It is important to prevent the problem in the first place.

When you are having difficulty getting going, motivate yourself by remembering the reasons that led you to freelancing in the first place. Think about how freelancing makes you feel and about the good things it allows you to have. For example, did the money you earned through freelancing let you buy your house or allow your children to get higher education?

Take time to celebrate and enjoy your hard work. Reward yourself with something that makes you happy as long as it is financially responsible. Rewarding yourself increases your feeling of accomplishment and helps keep your motivation up so you can do more and better.

SAMPLE SCENARIOS & MESSAGE TEMPLATES

In this section you will find sample message templates you can use for different scenarios. Each template contains basic elements that can be modified to suit the situation and your personality. Use each template individually or combine more than one to make up your messages. Where there are square brackets, provide the applicable information, select the appropriate choice, or replace with wording that applies to your situation.

In my correspondence I try to mirror the client's style of communication, use plenty of 'please' and 'thank you', and often include up to two smiley faces to express my friendliness. I address clients by the name they provided or their username and I use my first initial in my closing statement.

4.1 When you acknowledge an order that you can start

> *Thank you for your order and for sending everything I need to get started.*
>
> *I will keep you updated on the process. Please let me know if you have any questions.*

4.2 When you need time to respond

> *Please allow me some time to get back to you in [length of time] after I have a chance to [review your requirements / check into the matter / investigate further].*

4.3 When you ask for information

> *Would you please send me the following information so that I could [proceed / follow up / advise further]?*
>
> *[List of items and formats].*

4.4 When you ask for confirmation

Would you please confirm [my understanding / our agreement] as follows?

[List of items].

4.5 When you ask for clarification

To help me better understand [your requirement / your question / the issue], would you please clarify the following for me?

When you mentioned […], did you mean […]?

4.6 When you provide a quote

Based on your requirements, the cost would be [dollar amount] and [length of time] to do:

[List of items].

This quote includes [list of things that need to be done]. Additional costs may apply if the scope is changed.

Please let me know if you have any other questions or wish me to send an offer along.

4.7 When you decline work before an order is placed

I appreciate the opportunity to discuss this project with you, but after [reviewing / understanding / analyzing] your requirements, I believe that you will be better served by other sellers who can provide the exact service you need.

Thank you for your understanding and I hope you'd consider my service for other suitable projects.

4.8 When you decline work after an order is placed

Thank you for your order.

I appreciate your business very much, but after [reviewing / understanding / analyzing] your requirements, I believe that you will be better served by other sellers who can provide the exact service you need. Therefore, I will be sending a request for cancellation.

Thank you for your understanding and I hope you'd consider my service for other suitable projects.

4.9 When you offer samples

As per your request, attached please find a few samples of my work. Please let me know if you have any questions.

I'd love the opportunity to work with you and would gladly provide you a quote when you are ready to proceed.

4.10 When you offer free/trial work

Thank you for your interest in my service.

I am willing to do the following for you: [List of items and conditions].

Please let me know if this is acceptable to you and I will proceed accordingly.

4.11 When you don't offer free/trial work/samples

I wish I could provide you with the [free / trial work / samples] you requested, but that is not something I offer at this time.

Please review my portfolio at [website link] as it may provide the information you are looking for.

I'd love the opportunity to work with you and would gladly provide you a quote when you are ready to proceed.

4.12 When the client asks for proof that you can do the job

I fully understand your concern and wish to assure you that I can fulfill your requirements. After you order, I will work with you to make sure you are satisfied.

Please review my portfolio at [website link] that includes some of my past projects.

I'd love the opportunity to work with you and would gladly provide you a quote when you are ready to proceed.

4.13 When the client says he/she can't afford more

For the [dollar amount] you suggested, I will do this for you:

[List of items].

Please let me know if you'd like me to send an offer. I look forward to an opportunity to work with you.

4.14 When the client says your price is too high

I am sure you can find cheaper services and I wish to assure you that I will work with you to ensure that you will receive on time a quality product that fully meets your requirements.

Please let me know when you are ready to proceed. I look forward to an opportunity to work with you.

4.15 When you want to keep negotiating

I believe we're headed in the right direction. Let's find a way to make this work for both of us.

I look forward to our continuing work together.

4.16 When the client's offer is low before he/she orders

I wish I could do this for you for the amount you suggested, but based on your requirements, here are two options.

Option 1 – For the [dollar amount] you suggested and [length of time], I will do this for you:

[List of items].

Option 2 – For [dollar amount] and [length of time], I will do:

[List of items].

Please let me know which option you'd like me to send an offer for. I look forward to an opportunity to work with you.

4.17 When the client didn't pay enough on his/her order

Based on your requirements, here are two options:

Option 1 – For the [dollar amount] you paid, I will do this for you:

[List of items].

Option 2 – For [dollar amount] and [length of time], I will do:

[List of items].

If you wish to proceed with option 1, I will deliver by [date].

If you prefer option 2, please add the extra amount or let me know if you'd like me to send an offer to cover the difference. Otherwise, I would gladly cancel the order.

I look forward to your reply.

4.18 When the client wants to add or change an order

I would be happy to do […] for you for [dollar amount] and [length of time].

Please let me know if you'd like me to add this to the existing order or send a new offer.

4.19 When you want to add or change an order

I wanted to let you know that I really enjoy working with you.

As you know, the original scope has changed because of [reason(s)]. I'd like to discuss our options to either remove [requirement(s)] or add [dollar amount and/or time].

Please let me know your thoughts. I look forward to continuing our great working relationship.

4.20 When you want to ask for more money or time

I wanted to let you know that I really enjoy working with you.

Because of [reason(s)], I'd like to discuss with you the possibility of [adding [dollar amount] / extending the delivery time by [length of time]].

It is important to me to give you the best [service / product] so I really appreciate your consideration.

Please let me know your thoughts.

I look forward to continue our great working relationship.

4.21 When you provide status update on an order

I just wanted to let you know that I am working on your order. [Include specific details as needed.]

Everything is going well and according to schedule. I will do my best to deliver before the due date and I will let you know at once if any issues arise.

4.22 When you want to propose an idea

I thought about [proposal] and think it will [help your situation / fulfill your desire to…]. Please let me know your thoughts or if you wish me to send a quote for this.

4.23 When you deliver work

Your order is ready for your review and feedback. Please let me know if there is anything you'd like to change.

[Additional instructions if required].

4.24 When you follow up

Just following up to see if you had a chance to [get the information / send me the file / review the file I sent / review my proposal…].

Would you please let me know?

4.25 When the client points out your mistake

Thank you for [bringing this to my attention / raising the matter / pointing out the issue…].

It is important to me that I meet your expectations. I will get to it right away and will get back to you in [length of time].

4.26 When you want to apologize

Please accept my sincere apology for [the delayed response / not able to provide the information you were looking for / unable to get to] due to [unforeseen circumstances / an emergency / a personal matter].

4.27 When you need to resolve a dispute or conflict

I am so sorry that I may have misunderstood the [situation / issue / message / requirement].

According to […], my understanding is […].

At this point, we have the options to […] or […].

Would you please let me know which option you prefer?

I value our working relationship and would like to resolve this to your satisfaction.

4.28 When you want to express your gratitude

Thank you for [tip / review / message].

You've made my day and I really am grateful for your [generosity / trust / support].

4.29 When you ask for referrals

I am glad that you are happy with my [service / product]. If you know of someone that may be interested too, I'd really appreciate your referral.

Thank you very much for your support.

4.30 When you ask for feedback

Would you please provide your feedback on [...]?

Your feedback is important and I appreciate you taking the time. Thank you.

4.31 When you ask for a review

I really enjoyed working with you on this project.

Would you please rate and review the order for me? By letting others know about the quality and timely service you received, you are also helping me build my profile.

Thank you and I look forward to continue working with you in future projects.

4.32 When you ask for a review revision

> *Thank you for leaving a review.*
>
> *Your satisfaction is important to me and when I noticed that you indicated [...], I'd like to know if there is anything else I can do for you to get a better review. Would you please let me know? Thank you.*

4.33 When you cancel because the buyer is unresponsive

> *Since I haven't heard back from you, I am requesting a cancellation.*
>
> *I hope we have an opportunity to work together. Please get back to me when you are ready to proceed.*

4.34 When you cancel because you couldn't agree

> *Since we couldn't reach an agreement, I am requesting a cancellation.*
>
> *Thank you for the opportunity to discuss this with you. I am sorry that it didn't work out. All the best and I hope I can be of assistance in other projects.*

4.35 When you cancel because of insufficient fund

Since I haven't received the additional amount required for this order, I am requesting a cancellation.

When you are ready, please place another order for this project in the amount of [dollar amount] along with all the necessary information.

I look forward to an opportunity to work with you.

4.36 When you cancel because of out-of-scope work

I appreciate the opportunity to discuss this project with you, but it is not possible to fulfill your requirements at this time. Therefore, I am requesting a cancellation.

Thank you for your understanding and I hope you will consider my service for other suitable projects.

4.37 When you cancel because not enough information given

Since I haven't received the information required, I am requesting a cancellation.

When you are ready, please place another order with the necessary information.

I look forward to an opportunity to work with you.

4.38 When you cancel due to unforeseen circumstances

Due to [an unforeseen circumstance / an emergency / a personal matter…], I am requesting a cancellation as I will not able to complete this order in time for you.

Instead of rushing and delivering an inferior [product / service] to you, I'd rather cancel the order (which would affect my seller status).

I apologize for any inconvenience that this may cause. May I let you know once I am able to return to work?

Thank you for your understanding.

4.39 When you cancel at buyer's request

As per your request, I am requesting a cancellation.

Because cancellation affects my seller's rating, would you please contact me prior to ordering in the future?

Thank you for your co-operation. I hope to get an opportunity to work with you.

4.40 When you cancel because the buyer complains

Thank you for your feedback.

We agreed that the end product is [...] which I delivered after spending time to [list of items] based on your requirements.

I value our working relationship and your satisfaction is important to me. But since we've exhausted our options, I am requesting a cancellation even though I've completed the work.

Please let me know if there is anything else I can do for you.

4.41 When you cancel duplicate orders

I am requesting cancellation of this order because it is a duplicate of [order number].

Please accept the cancellation request to get the money back into your account.

I will communicate with you through [order number].

4.42 When someone asks for help that you can give

Thank you for reaching out and I'm happy to help!

[Provide details].

All the best and please let me know if I can be of further assistance.

4.43 When someone asks for help that you can't give

Thank you for your message.

I'd love to help. Unfortunately, I [don't have the expertise / am unable to at this time] to give the help you need.

[Provide suggestions if possible].

All the best.

4.44 When you ask for help

I'm looking for […] that I was hoping you could help with.

Would you please let me know or direct me to the appropriate person or place for this? I appreciate your assistance.

Thank you.

4.45 When you ask for suggestions

I am working on improving my [website / profile / presentation…]. Would you please take a look at [URL / attachment…] and suggest ways to make it better?

I value your opinion and appreciate you taking the time to do this for me. Thank you very much.

4.46 When you provide feedback

After a [thorough assessment / careful consideration] of your [suggestion / idea…], I believe it's going [to work / not work] because […]. I am [glad / afraid] that this [will / will not] provide the result you expect.

I am available to discuss further, if you wish.

4.47 When you postpone a request for action

I wish I could do this for you right away, but I am currently working with other clients ahead of you. Thank you for your patience and understanding.

4.48 When you explain your process

The [product / service] I provide requires me to [list of items / tools / processes / amount of time…].

Without getting into the working details, I know sometimes it's hard to see what is involved. I hope my explanation helps you better understand the value behind the [product / service] you receive from me.

Downloadable Item
4 Sample scenarios & message templates **Log in:** https://goo.gl/MXjBmM or **Sign up:** https://goo.gl/xpPbNM

REFERENCES

COMMON QUESTIONS AND SUGGESTIONS

5.1 Managing business

Q1. How would I find out more about the business side of freelancing, for example, business registration and other requirements such as taxes and insurance?

Prepare your list of questions then research using the Internet, visit government agencies and local associations, and connect with other freelancers and small business owners.

Q2. How would I know whether my freelancing business is successful or not?

You need to define what success means to you. You can only measure your success when you have clear and measurable goals which are unique to you. Your goals need to be time-sensitive and quantitative. Be as specific as possible. For example, if you measure success financially, some of your goals maybe "to earn $5,000 a month starting next month" or "by the end of next month, find two clients who pay more than $500 per order." If you measure success by time, perhaps your goals are "to get a one-month vacation in August next year" or "to work only 5 hours a day in May, June, and July." You will then know if you are successful depending on whether or not you reach your goals.

Q3. As a new freelancer, what are the top three common mistakes that I should learn to avoid?

Since freelancing income is irregular, don't treat it as net profit that you can spend without reservation. You need to put aside money for all business expenses such as taxes, accounting, and other operational costs.

It's difficult to decide what to charge for a project at the beginning so you may let the clients dictate the price. Some clients use the "limited budget" as a reason, promise to give more or repeat business, or even threaten to purchase the service somewhere else to get you to do the work at the price they want. It's your job to charge a fair price that reflects the value you provide. Also, you need to figure out your lowest acceptable rate—the amount below which you absolutely will not work. Having this figured out will help you make the right decisions when you're tempted to take on anything that comes along. See sections 2.5 and 2.8 on how to price your service. And when you find a client whose budget does not meet your worth, it's up to you to decide whether or not that client can afford your services.

You will be tempted to accept every offer that comes your way, especially when work is scarce. Saying "yes" to everything will leave you busy doing low-paying work. Say "no" to projects that are not a good match. Doing so will give you more time and creative energy to invest in those projects that excite you and pay you better.

Q4. How do I know if I am charging enough for my service?

Freelance rates are subjective, but if you cannot pay your bills, can't meet current deadlines comfortably, or you have no time for new clients or your life, you're probably not charging enough.

Q5. As a new freelancer, how do I figure out what part of the process I've done wrong after I set up my profile but get no business?

When you first start out, it's going to take some time to get business. You need to give yourself time to succeed. Be patient and ask other freelancers for advice and feedback without sounding needy and desperate.

If you don't even get inquiries, it is likely that people can't find you or they decide not to contact you. Check your description, keywords, and category to make sure your profile stands out in the appropriate places. Follow the suggestions in sections 2.4 to 2.7 plus these tips:

- Upload a high-resolution head shot with a pleasant smile.

- Showcase your skills through your portfolio. If your skills are difficult to prove online, ask for recommendations from previous employers or clients to be quoted online.
- Offer only something you have real world experience with.
- Price your service reasonably to match your experience and to show confidence in the quality. Cheaper is not always better.

If you get inquires but no sales, check to see if you've been communicating your expectations realistically and appropriately in a timely manner.

Take this slow time to do some marketing activities to promote your service.

Q6. What are some marketing activities I can do?

Set up a list of marketing activities and do any one of them each day. For example:

- Update your portfolio with better and current samples.
- Update your social media network profiles.
- Post your service on social media networks.

- Tell people you know about your service.
- Send a message to your past clients, asking for referrals.
- Apply for buyer's requests for jobs in your specific field.
- Participate in a forum discussion.
- Set up a pay-per-click ad.
- Write a blog post for your website.
- Write a guest blog post.

5.2 Dealing with clients

Q7. How do I identify and deal with difficult clients effectively?

Every freelancer encounters difficult clients from time to time. Difficult clients monopolize your time, make unreasonable demands, and frustrate you. They often come with some warning signs that you use to identify and deal with each type. Remember you can't please everyone and sometimes it is necessary to let clients go. Following are 15 types of client and the number in the brackets is the section where you can find the suggested message template to use for each type.

1. For those who are unsure of what they want and change their minds constantly, clearly outline in writing everything and reject demands that divert from that. (4.17)
2. For those who insist on getting more out of you each time by expanding the scope of the project, give them an option to buy the out-of-scope work. (4.18)
3. For those who lack the awareness of how much work and time is required, explain the process to them. (4.48)
4. For those who think they are your only client and deserve 100 percent of your time, establish clear timelines and provide updates to show you are on track. (4.21)
5. For those who are inconsistent in keeping their priorities and timelines, get an agreement as soon as possible and stick to it so that you don't endanger other clients' projects. (4.4)
6. For those who don't provide clear information in a timely manner with the expectation that you will do

whatever you think is best, get their agreement before any major work involved. (4.4)

7. For those who are rigid in their approach and leave little room for your ideas, get a clear understanding of what they are trying to accomplish and tell them truthfully when their approach won't work. (4.46)
8. For those who may not know what they want but are certain on what they don't want, tell them they need to give you exact requirements before you spend more time discussing. (4.3)
9. For those who are extremely concerned about their budget, get agreement on the scope based on their budget and stick to it. (4.4)
10. For those who have unrealistic expectations, don't be afraid to refuse if what they want will take too much of a toll on you. (4.43)
11. For those who tend to latch onto tiny details, instead of asking them what they preferences are, ask them what they want to achieve and help them achieve

their goal. If they are still not happy about the result, be prepared to let them go. (4.34)

12. For those who believe that they can do what you do quicker or cheaper, tell them why the things they want cost time or money. (4.48)
13. For those who have to consult others before making any decisions, get them to agree on a go or no-go due date. (4.4)
14. For those who are non-responsive for a long period then bombard you with requests that need to be done immediately, tell them that you have a process where all requests go into a queue to ensure that every client is treated respectfully and fairly. (4.47)
15. For those who praise your completed work but decide they want something completely different, make it clear that additional costs may apply if what they want is out of the original quote. (4.6)

Q8. How do I deal with an unhappy client?

When a client politely says you didn't deliver what he/she was expecting and his/her expectations are not unrealistic or unreasonable, do everything in your power to satisfy him/her. This may mean you need to spend more time or get less money. It is important to keep your client happy and your reputation intact.

Q9. How do I recognize when refusing a project is in the best interest of both parties?

Many freelancers have trouble refusing projects because they fear saying no to money they need. But when you are not excited about the project or the client, don't have the right skill set, or the project doesn't contribute to your business or portfolio, refusing a project is in the best interest of both parties.

Q10. What should I do when I know what the client wants won't work?

Explain why you think what the client wants won't work and offer an alternate solution. This shows your expertise and care. Your client will be especially grateful when your suggestion turns out well.

5.3 Developing skills

Q11. What skills do I need to develop while I am growing my business?

While you'll spend the bulk of your time working on orders and communicating with clients, carve out time to learn new skills and upgrade existing ones. Other than improving your technical and soft skills, you will need to learn business skills and be aware of new technologies and changes that may affect you and your business. The remaining time you'll spend on learning how to be more efficient in marketing activities and other administrative tasks such as planning, bookkeeping, and organizing your workspace.

Q12. How do I overcome procrastination?

If you suffer from persistent procrastination, seek the advice of a trained health professional to rule it out as a cause of serious stress and illness. Otherwise, procrastination is an embedded habit that you probably can't break overnight. Try different strategies to give yourself the best possible chance of succeeding. To make you feel more in control, instead of thinking "I need or have to do this," think "I choose to do this." Write down the tasks that you need to complete, and specify a time for doing them. Tackle tasks as soon as they arise so they don't build up. When you work, avoid distraction as much as possible. Get the tasks you find least pleasant out of the way early. If you complete a task on time, reward yourself with a treat. You may also want to ask someone to hold you accountable by checking up on you.

Q13. What if I make a mistake?

All of us make mistakes and we can't avoid them all. When you do, accept responsibility and do everything you can to fix your mistake. Figure out what you can do to avoid it in the future or how to succeed next time.

COMMONLY MISUSED WORDS

The following are examples of commonly misused words to avoid so that your written communication reflects professionalism. Keep a list of misused words and words you are having difficulty with close by for reference.

Accept = Agree to or receive	**Except** = Leave out
Adverse = Detrimental	**Averse** = Disinclined
Advice = Guidance or recommendations as in "My advice"	**Advise** = Suggest, recommend, or inform as in "I advise"
Affect = To influence as in "this affects that"	**Effect** = An influence as in "that is an effect of this"
Allude = Suggest or call attention to indirectly	**Elude** = Evade or escape
Among = 3 or more as in "among friends"	**Between** = 2 only as in "you and me"
Appraise = Ascertain	**Apprise** = Inform
Bring = Transport to here	**Take** = Transport to elsewhere
Can = Has the ability	**May** = Has permission

Capital = Important city or wealth	**Capitol** = The building for lawmaking
Complement = Completes or brings to perfection	**Compliment** = A polite expression of praise or admiration
Compose = To make up	**Comprise** = To include
Credible = Believable, trustworthy	**Credulous** = Gullible
Depreciate = Decrease	**Deprecate** = Disparage
Ensure = To make certain	**Insure** = To secure or protect
Explicit = Stated clearly and in detail	**Implicit** = Implied though not plainly expressed
Farther = Refers to physical distance	**Further** = Describes the degree or extent of an action or situation
Fewer = Refers to separate items that can be counted as in "fewer dollars"	**Less** = Refers to a whole as in "less money"
Imply = Suggest something	**Infer** = Draw a conclusion

without saying	from what someone else implies
It's = It is	**Its** = Belonging to or associate with a child, animal, or thing
Lead = To guide someone towards something	**Led** = Past tense of "lead"
Loose = Unbound or not tight	**Lose** = To not win or to misplace
Mitigate = Alleviate	**Militate** = Provide reasons for
Passed = Moved or caused to move	**Past** = Gone by in time and no longer existing
Precede = To go before	**Proceed** = To continue
Principal = First in the order of importance or a sum of money invested or lent	**Principle** = A belief, philosophy, or fundamental truth
Sight = A view or a glimpse	**Site** = A location
Than = For comparison as in "shorter than"	**Then** = Sequence in time as in "now and then"
There = Place or position	**Their** = Belonging to or associate with people or things

Threw = Past tense of "throw"	**Through** = Moving in from one side and out the other or continuing in time
To = Motion in a direction or identify the person or thing affected as in "from here to there"	**Too** = Also or a higher degree than desirable as in "I like it too" or "too hot"
Weather = State of the atmosphere	**Whether** = Introduces an alternative
Were = Past tense of "are"	**Where** = A place
Who's = "Who is" or "Who has"	**Whose** = Belonging to or associated with which person
You're = "You are"	**Your** = Belonging to or associate with you

USEFUL LINKS

- **50 Legitimate Ways to Make Money from Home** – https://scottalanturner.com/50-legitimate-ways-to-make-money-from-home-in-2016
- **50 Tips for Starting Your Own Company** – https://www.entrepreneur.com/article/235903
- **A Simple 6-Step Process to Starting a Small Business** – https://www.entrepreneur.com/article/248802
- **Amazon S3** http://aws.amazon.com – Provides secure and highly scalable space for storing and retrieving data from anywhere.
- **Dictionary** http://www.dictionary.com – A website and app where you can look up words in a dictionary.
- **Dropbox** http://dropbox.com – Provides storage for files that can be shared and viewed on any device.
- **Google Alerts** http://google.com/alerts – Monitors and sends e-mail updates on the topics you choose, for example, when someone mentions your name or your book.
- **Google Drive** http://drive.google.com – Provides storage for files that can be shared.

- **Google Keep** http://google.com/keep – Keeps lists, pictures, and notes synced across all your devices.
- **How to Setup a Fiverr Gig Like a Pro!** https://www.youtube.com/watch?v=D6yb8XgdK4s.
- **Hemingway Editor** http://www.hemingwayapp.com – A tool to help make your writing clearer.
- **Mention** http://mention.com – Tracks and sends alerts of the topics you follow.
- **Mint** – Allows you to create and track and monitor a budget https://www.mint.com.
- **OneDrive** http://onedrive.live.com – Provides storage for files that can be accessed on phone, tablet, or computer.
- **Pick the Brain** http://www.pickthebrain.com/blog – A collection of self-improvement articles focusing on productivity, motivation and confidence.
- **Pocket** https://getpocket.com – A researching tool to collect and manage your digital library that allows you to save articles, videos or pretty much anything so you can view later.

- **Rescue Time** https://www.rescuetime.com – Time tracker tool that helps you understand your daily habits so you can focus and be more productive.
- **SMRecorder** http://www.video2down.com/smrecorder.php – A simple and free desktop audio/video recorder that captures desktop video and audio, camera, and microphone inputs. You can add onscreen annotation and narration.
- **Shoeboxed** https://www.shoeboxed.com – Allows you to photograph receipts and store and organize them online.
- **Todoist** http://en.todoist.com – Task management software that facilitates collaboration.
- **Toggl** https://www.toggl.com – Time tracker tool to track the time it takes to complete various tasks. Toggl also lets you look at reports and see how much time you spent on different projects throughout the week.
- **Wave** https://www.waveapps.com – A cloud-based invoicing, accounting, payroll, payments, and personal finance app.
- **Zapier** https://zapier.com – Automation for moving information between many common web apps.

MAY YOU BE A SUCCESSFUL FREELANCER

Thank you for allowing me to share my knowledge and experiences with you. I am glad I discovered that a freelancing business is a viable option for me if I want to continue after retirement. I hope it is a good option for you too for the purpose that you are pursuing.

Although freelancing is a lifestyle that provides a sense of freedom unlike any 9 to 5 job, it is something you really have to want and be prepared to work for. There isn't a single piece of magical advice that will make you an instant success. Keep on learning. Knowing how to best apply who you are and what you know to what you want to do will make you successful.

While money matters, it is my sincere hope that you don't let it define who you are. When you balance your time between building your business relationships and building your personal relationships, you will enjoy a balanced and happy life that you earn and deserve.

I'd love to hear your story as to how this book has helped you on your path to becoming a successful freelancer. I would also appreciate it if you'd post a short review for this book. Your review is an invaluable tool to let other readers know what to expect and help them decide whether this book would be of use to them. It will help me to make continuous improvements based on your comments and suggestions as well. Would you please take a few seconds to let your social networking friends know about this book if you think they would benefit from it? Thank you.

Please feel free to reach out to me at vvcam@because.zone if I can be of further assistance to you in any way.

Blessings to you and I wish you tons of fun and success on your freelancing journey!

V.

ACKNOWLEDGEMENTS

Thank you to Fiverr.com and all my clients there. Without you, this book simply would not exist.

Thank you to all the readers of my previous books, for giving me the motivation to continue writing. Your support gives purpose and encouragement to the words between these pages.

Thank you to my daughter, Candace, for putting my words and ideas through good tests. You continue to awe me with your young wisdom and I am proud of who you've become.

To the Quiethouse Editing team of beta readers, Jessica Lovelace and Kirsty McManus, thank you for your keen observations and constructive suggestions to make the book better. Thank you, Starr Waddell, for continuously deliver your professional service with a smile.

To my editor, David Loving from davidaloving.com, thank you for your amazing ability to say more with less and make everything clearer and better.

Thank you to my husband, Jack, for always being incredibly supportive. I thrive and succeed because of you.

ABOUT THE AUTHOR

V.V. and her family had to flee Vietnam by boat when she was just at the tender age of 13. When most young girls at that age would have been worrying about acne and boys, she was living in Hong Kong, housed in a prison that had been turned into an overcrowded refugee camp.

That was where she started her journey to become the happy and successful wife, mother, and entrepreneur that she is today. While working in an electronics factory earning money to help her family survive the hardships of daily life, she taught herself to read and write Chinese. A year later, a church sponsored her family to start their new life in a small town in Ontario, Canada.

She put her language learning skills to use again, this time mastering English. She soon became one of the top students at her school and helped the office staff with her typing and office skills. Along with her industrious family, she learned to sew and made money sewing for local shops and for friends.

Her resume soon included an impressive list of accomplishments: She worked her way from seamstress, waitress, bartender, and receptionist to IT support specialist and trainer, to real estate agent and broker. She has worked in executive positions with large organizations managing finances, human resources, and relationships and has built a couple of small businesses.

In her spare time, she created two high-traffic and successful websites that offer teaching tools and support to the Vietnamese communities. She's also founded a philanthropic organization that provides micro loans for poor people in Vietnam.

V. V. Cam lives in Toronto, Canada with her family.

BOOKS BY V.V. CAM

http://www.because.zone/books-by-v-v-cam

Because Self-Publishing Works Series:

Everything I Learned About How to Publish a Book

Everything I Learned About How to Market a Book

http://www.because.zone/because-self-publishing-works

The two books in the Because Self-Publishing Works series share the knowledge V. V. Cam learned while helping her husband publish and market his book, **because** *– a novel by Jack A. Langedijk http://www.because.zone.*

Because Money Matters Series:

The 8 Principles to Build Your Wealth

How to Earn More Money as a Freelancer in a Gig Economy

(http://www.because.zone/because-money-matters)

Because Money Matters: The 8 Principles to Build Your Wealth starts the series with the lessons V. V. Cam learned from her mother on managing personal finance.

INDEX

NOTES

NOTES

NOTES

NOTES

NOTES

NOTES

NOTES

Made in the USA
Las Vegas, NV
23 November 2021